Hands Across Africa

Hands
Across Africa

Joanne De Jonge
and Marjo Rouw

BAKER BOOK HOUSE
Grand Rapids, Michigan 49516

Copyright 1988 by Baker Book House Company

ISBN: 0-8010-2988-0

Second printing, July 1989

Printed in the United States of America

Contents

Preface

The Hand of God

Many people have had a hand in the creation of this book.

Originally, Marian Schoolland began the work. She intended to introduce Christian children in the United States and Canada to the Church's mission activity in other parts of the world. That introduction, she hoped, would stimulate interest in missions.

The most important purpose of that introduction, however, was to show that the hand of God reaches to all parts of the earth and touches the lives of all his children. To do this, she decided to relate true stories of children on the mission field, children of both missionaries and local people. The theme of the stories was to be the wonderful care that God shows all his children.

Many missionaries contributed to the work. Some home on leave, some retired, and some overseas sent stories about themselves or about others. Some sent outlines of main events, which Marian crafted into stories. Others sent ideas that she incorporated into other stories. Still others sent their stories fully written, which she edited slightly. Most of the stories, she found, were set in Nigeria. So she concentrated on that country, and the book began to take form.

But God called Marian home to heaven before the book was completed.

Joanne De Jonge fell heir to the work. She edited more stories, filled in more outlines, incorporated more ideas, and tried to pull it together. But she felt a lack because she had never been to Nigeria. So she called for help.

Marjo Rouw answered that call. Having grown up in Nigeria and just recently returned to the United States, she provided the missing authentic details and helped bring life to the work. She wrote many of the stories herself and had a hand in editing all the others. She served as primary contributor, authority on things Nigerian, and consultant on dozens of details.

Through all of this, Dick Eppinga of Christian Reformed World Missions served as the glue that held the project together. The only person who saw the work from the birth of the idea to the publication of this book, he kept it alive. Through his office he helped gather stories, relay messages, and move materials. He brought people together and helped transfer the project from one hand to another. And he provided both the impulse and the encouragement to complete this book.

Any of the people who had a hand in this book would be quick to tell you that they did not do it alone, nor were they the primary source. Every person who worked on this project can testify that God was the one source who truly guided it and saw it to completion. Each of us has felt his hand in this work.

And so you see before you a book of many stories from many sources. If you wonder about those sources, the list at the back of the book will name names. But it is one book, guided by one source, with one message. We pray that you will see the hand of God at work in the stories told here, and that you will feel his hand in yours.

1

Kpa Se Nongo

It will be difficult," the girls said. *"Kpa se nongo (but we'll try)."*

The girls were students at a mission boarding school in Sevav, Nigeria. Mr. Terpstra, a missionary there, had asked them to consider a special project. "Would you let one more girl come to live with you?" he had asked.

"Of course," they had answered at once. "Why do you ask?"

"This girl is special," he had explained. "She's not like a normal Tiv girl. Her mind has not grown as the mind of a normal child grows. She will not be able to learn easily. And she does not behave well. It will be difficult for you to live with her.

"She is also an orphan," Mr. Terpstra had continued. "Maybe she really has no father or mother. Or perhaps her parents don't want her because she is not normal. We don't know. But we do know that she is an unhappy little girl with no name and no place to live. Will you take her to live with you?"

So the girls discussed the matter. "She may give us trouble," one girl said.

"Can we live with a girl like that?" another asked.

"We will have to teach her many things," still another said, "if we can."

One girl summed it up very well: "It will be very difficult."

"What would Jesus want us to do?" they began to ask each other. "If we love Jesus, we should do what he says."

"He says that we should love one another," they decided. "We should try to help each other."

And that's when they said, "It will be difficult, *kpa se nongo (but we will try)."*

When Tiv people say, *"Kpa se nongo,"* they usually mean, "We'll give it our best effort and we'll stay with it as long as we can." That's just what the girls at Sevav meant. They tackled their new job with willingness, and they accepted the nameless little girl with love.

The first few days with the new girl at school were difficult. She had many things to learn. She didn't know how to do any chores. All of the girls at Sevav had to help with chores.

"This is how you must sweep," one girl told her. She took a grass broom and showed the new girl just how to sweep each hut. But the new girl couldn't learn easily, and had to be shown again and again.

"Kpa se nongo," the girls reminded each other. "We will try."

"You must wash your uniform and keep it clean," her new friends told her. But she did not know how to scrub her dress in a bucket of cold water and lay it on the grass to dry in the sun.

"Kpa se nongo," the girls told each other. "Remember, we will try."

"You must help fetch buckets of water from the well," she was told. But the new girl did not know how to draw water or balance the heavy bucket on her head. She had to be shown again and again.

"You also must help prepare meals," one girl instructed. She showed the new girl just how to chop firewood and pound yams. But the new girl couldn't learn easily, and had to be shown again and again.

Again the girls said to each other, "*Kpa se nongo.* We will try to love her and help her. We will try to show Jesus' love. *Kpa se nongo.*"

That's how the little girl was named. The other girls began to call her Kpasenongo. They weren't teasing her with that name. They were reminding themselves that they had said, "But we'll try." Kpasenongo liked that name, so it became her name.

And so Kpasenongo became one of the girls at Sevav. At first she was unhappy. She didn't smile much and she did have a lot of trouble learning. But the other girls were very patient and very kind. They tried very hard. Soon Kpasenongo began to smile. And she began to try. And she began to learn.

At times she had to learn the hard way. That's what happened when she forgot to take her daily shower.

One of the girls had shown Kpasenongo just how to shower. "Take this gourd dipper," the girl had said, showing her a gourd hollowed out to hold water. "Dip it into this bucket of cold water, and then pour the water over yourself. We must shower like this every day. It's very important."

So Kpasenongo took her cold shower every day, just as the other girls did. But one day she forgot.

"Kpasenongo, did you take your shower?"

"No. I forgot."

"Then you know what you must do tonight?"

"No, I do not."

"You must sleep in a separate hut by yourself. You may not sleep in a hut with the other girls!"

That was a very severe punishment for a Tiv girl. Tiv people love to be near each other. They grow up with lots of people around them all the time, and they like it that way. All the girls always slept in the same hut so that they could be near each other. To sleep in a separate hut was indeed a punishment.

"Kpasenongo, we must do the same thing if we forget to shower," the other girls assured her. "We will all be here for you tomorrow."

And they were. Day after day, month after month, they helped Kpasenongo. They never tired of teaching her and helping her learn. Gradually they forgot that they were helping her. As the months passed, Kpasenongo's happiness grew and some of her problems faded. She loved the people at Sevav because they loved her, and she tried to do her best for them. Gradually, Kpasenongo became like the other girls at Sevav.

The time came for Mr. Terpstra to leave Sevav. But he didn't worry about the once-nameless, unhappy little girl he had asked the others to take in. He knew that the other girls had promised, *"Kpa se nongo."*

One day, several years later, Mr. Terpstra visited a Nigerian village far away from Sevav. There he met a woman who was married and had a child. A smile lit her face, and she glowed with happiness as she spoke to him. She told him how happy she was with her very own family and how well she took care of them. If he hadn't recognized her, he never would have guessed that she had once been an unhappy little girl with many problems. That woman was Kpasenongo!

"It will be difficult," the girls of Sevav had said. *"Kpa se nongo."* The girls of Sevav didn't only try; they succeeded splendidly in showing the love of Jesus.

Two Old Women and Two Small Yams

"Cock-a-doodle-doo!"

David rolled over in bed, sleepily pulled open his mosquito net, and groped for the alarm clock standing on a chair nearby. He pushed the alarm button to "off" before the clock could start ringing. Those dumb old roosters! A person didn't even need an alarm clock with them around. They were always crowing and scratching near his window, often long before it was time to get up. But David could hear his father listening to the 6:30 mission-radio broadcast in the living room, so he knew it was time to rise and shine.

Well, one good thing about getting up early, even though it was school vacation, was that the weather was nice and cool. By midday it would be sweltering hot and humid again. Then no one would feel like doing anything but sitting inside, close to a fan, with an ice-cold drink.

Even that wasn't always possible. The electricity went off so often that a person couldn't depend on it for anything. Why, they had to eat supper by candlelight the

14

last four evenings. And Mother had said that the last three washdays had been a disaster: the electricity kept going off halfway through her wash. Of course, the washing machine couldn't run without electricity.

"This country!" grumbled David, who lived with his brother, sister and missionary parents in Nigeria. "Hot and sticky, noisy roosters, off-and-on electricity, no candy stores, no McDonald's. I wish we were back in America!" And feeling quite sorry for himself, he climbed out of his mosquito net. In a few minutes he was dressed in a pair of cool shorts, a tank top and rubber thongs. "Well, at least I don't have to wear a lot of clothes here," he mumbled to himself.

Breakfast didn't seem to improve David's bad mood. "Yuck! Powdered milk again?" he grumbled. "Mom, do I have to eat these Rice Krispies? They're so stale. And look! There's a weevil floating in my bowl. Boy! What I wouldn't give for some Froot Loops!"

"David, that's enough of your complaining," said Dad sternly. Then he added, hoping to change David's bad mood, "You might be interested to know that Dr. Kremer is going to visit the leprosy hospital today. She has invited you to go along with her. I think you are old enough to behave yourself." Dad set his coffee cup down and looked at David with a twinkle in his eye.

"I'd love to go!" David always enjoyed doing things with Dr. Kremer. She was usually very busy either at the large mission hospital in Mkar or making medical visits to villages and clinics in the countryside. Yet, knowing the boy's interest in medical work and his dream of becoming a doctor someday, she often took the time to tell an interesting bit of hospital news. And sometimes she invited David to go with her on a medical visit.

David had never been to the leprosy hospital. He knew that leprosy was no longer the dread disease it had been in Jesus' day. There was now medicine that could cure leprosy. But many Nigerian people with leprosy often waited too long to go to the hospital for help. Then, because of the disease, they would begin to lose parts of their fingers and toes.

"The leprosy hospital is really doing several things," explained Dr. Kremer as they bumped along in her grey, hospital Land Rover. "First, the leprosy patients are given medicine to stop the disease from getting worse. Then, trained therapists help patients learn to walk again with special shoes, crutches or braces. And finally, the patients are taught to make useful things, which will help them earn a little bit of money."

David was happy that Dr. Kremer had some time to show him around. He watched with great interest as several boys about his own age struggled to walk back and forth between two wooden handrails. Their leg braces looked hot and uncomfortable. David quietly thanked God for his own two sturdy legs.

He was fascinated to watch another man with only stumps for feet expertly work a large weaving loom. Back and forth, back and forth went the wooden shuttle. He loved the bright blue color of the cloth the man was weaving. Nearby, three men sat on the cement floor weaving grass baskets. All of them were missing parts of fingers. Yet they rapidly wove long strips of grass together as if a person didn't really need ten fingers. David uncomfortably hid his ten healthy fingers behind his back.

"I want to check on a tablecloth I have ordered," said Dr. Kremer. "Then we must be on our way." They

stepped into another room where several ladies sat
working on beautiful delicate embroidery.

"*M'sugh, Maman,*" David greeted a kindly old woman
in the proper respectful way. "How do you do such lovely
work? You have no fingers!"

The old woman's laugh revealed several empty holes
between yellow-orange teeth. David knew she had been
enjoying kola nuts, a favorite Nigerian snack. They
make your teeth orange if you eat lots of them. "My
boy," she said, "you have to use what God gives you!"

Back in the Land Rover, David wiped the sweat drip-
ping down his forehead. "The leprosy village is close,"
explained Dr. Kremer, "but we'll drive there, as it's getting too hot to walk." David agreed.

It was fun driving on roads like this! Tall elephant
grass stood higher than the car on either side. The only
sign of a road was the set of narrow tracks through the
grass. Tall grass even grew between the tracks. Their
progress was slow, as they kept meeting people on motor-
cycles, bicycles, and on foot. Many of them were carrying heavy loads on their heads and babies on their
backs. "Probably on their way to market," thought David.

Soon they reached the circle of mud huts, which as
in most Tiv villages were surrounded by smooth, neatly
swept earth. Scrawny chickens scratched in the dirt. A
few goats rested lazily in the shade of a mango tree.
David didn't like the looks of a mangy yellow dog slink-
ing around them, so he kept close to Dr. Kremer.

The visitors were greeted warmly by the lepers living
in the village. David thought he had never seen such a
pitiful group. They looked very poor and wore tattered,
faded clothes. He saw where they had lost parts or all
of their fingers and toes, their deformed feet and swollen

legs. "It's a good thing I'm here and not my sister," he thought. "She can't stand to see such things!"

The lepers knew Dr. Kremer well, for she had visited them before. They enjoyed hearing her speak in their own Tiv language; many laughed with pleasure.

Two old women approached the white visitors for a closer look. They were both carrying small wooden hoes over their shoulders. They looked hot, tired, and dirty. David knew they had just come from working in their yam fields.

The first old woman seemed rather unhappy and cross. "*U ngu nana* (How are you)?" asked Dr. Kremer.

The old woman looked at David and said, "I am not very well. This strong young man should go into my fields and work. I am too old and tired. My body is sick. I should not have to work hard like this for my food." And she turned and hobbled off, feeling quite unhappy with herself and with everyone else.

The other old woman, however, was much different. "Come with me," she invited the visitors, with a friendly smile. They followed her into a small round mud hut.

It was very dark inside and smelled like smoke. The grass roof overhead protected the old woman from both the rain and the sun. It actually was quite cool inside the hut.

When his eyes grew accustomed to the dim light, David looked around him. The walls were blackened from the smoke of the old woman's cooking fire in the center of the hut. A small grass mat lay on the floor; that must be her bed. Several round metal basins lay toward the back of the hut. Each held a different food from the woman's farm.

The old woman quickly offered the visitors two short stools. Then she squatted comfortably on the floor. She reached for a small basket about half full of peanuts and passed them to her guests.

"Yum," thought David as he munched happily. He loved peanuts. He knew that they, too, were from the old woman's farm.

As David listened to the two women chatting together in the Tiv language, his thoughts turned to the old woman. She was, no doubt, a mother and a grandmother of many children. Yet she was alone. She obviously lived a hard life. She worked hard on her small farm, growing all she needed to eat. Yet she was happy. David could tell that by looking at her face. And he knew why. She was a Christian. She knew and loved the Lord Jesus. That made all the difference.

When they rose to leave, they thanked the old woman warmly for her kindness. She bent over a small pile of seven or eight yams. Picking up one in each hand, she hobbled toward her visitors. With a broad smile she handed one to each of them.

David stepped out of the dark, dingy hut holding his small yam. He squinted in the brightness of the hot African sun. They said goodbye to the old woman and walked back to the Land Rover.

As they bounced toward home, David was unusually quiet. He had a lot to think about after that day.

"I am a lot like that other old woman," he said to himself. "I complain about my problems and forget to be patient and kind to the people around me, especially my own family."

He knew he would never forget the difference that Jesus' love made in the second old woman. She had hardly anything, yet she shared generously with her guests. "Those were not the two smallest yams, either," he thought. "She gave us her best."

"Well, David my boy," said Dad later that evening as they sat together eating supper. "How was your day?"

David laid down his fork. He looked at his ten healthy fingers. He swung his two strong legs. He looked at the bowl of cooked mashed yams and at the other delicious food on the table. Through new eyes he saw his cheerful comfortable home and his loving family around him.

"You know, Dad," he said slowly, "I'll never forget this day. I never realized how much I have to be thankful for. And I will never forget the lesson I learned from two old women and two small yams."

3

≣ Josie

Will you take a baby into your home for a little while?" No one knew how important those words were for Josie.

Josie was born in a missionary hospital in Takum, Nigeria. Her mother had been very ill before Josie was born, so when Josie arrived she was small and weak. After a few weeks, Josie was still struggling to survive.

"Her mother is very ill again and cannot care for the baby. The hospital is crowded and we're all very busy," Nurse Julie said. "This baby needs extra loving care. Will you take her home for a little while?"

Dianne, a missionary mother, didn't have to think for very long. She had taken other babies into her home. Her own young daughters loved to help care for the babies.

"Of course," she replied quickly. "If we can help her, bring her to our house."

So Josie was brought to live with Dianne and her family. She was so tiny that she slept in a laundry hamper. But she began to thrive under the love and attention she received. She opened her big brown eyes and stared at everything around her. She began to gurgle and smile sweetly at anyone who looked into her hamper or played with her. Within one week, Josie had taken a turn for the better. Perhaps she could survive, the missionaries thought, and even soon return to her Nigerian family.

But, less than two weeks after Josie moved into the mission home, a stranger showed up at their front door. He was a Nigerian, of the Tiv tribe. "I am the baby's father," the stranger said. "My name is Orya. I am most grateful that you have taken care of my daughter. But now my wife, the baby's mother, has died. I cannot care for the child. Would you kindly keep my child until I can find another woman who can care for her?"

"Oh, yes," the family agreed. They nodded their heads and smiled so that the man would understand. "We will care for Josie until you have found a woman."

Several times during the next weeks, Orya came to greet the missionary family and to see his daughter. But each time, he said, "I have not found a woman to care for my daughter."

When Josie was four months old, Orya came for a special visit. "I cannot find a woman to care for my daughter," he said. "I have come to ask you for special help. If you would please take care of her for me until she is twelve years old I would be most grateful. I will take her back when she is twelve years old."

"Oh, dear, that would not be fair to Josie," the missionaries said. "After twelve years she will be used to our way of living. Then it will be very difficult for her to return to her own people. Already Josie recognizes us and is happy when she is near us. After twelve years she will love us too much to leave us. And we love her already. How could we send her away after she has lived with us for twelve years?"

So they tried to make Orya understand. It was very

important that he find someone to take care of Josie very soon. It would not be fair to her to let her stay for so long and then take her away.

"We will come to your compound in a few weeks," they said. "We will visit you to see how you are doing." Orya left, and Josie stayed with the family.

A few weeks later the whole family took Josie and piled into their car. They bumped along over a dusty road full of potholes for several hours before they reached Orya's village.

When they arrived, all the village people came out to greet the family. They brought chairs so that their special guests could sit down. Orya proudly held his daughter. Everyone in the crowd admired Josie and wanted to take turns holding her. Everyone talked quickly and excitedly in Tiv, which the missionaries did not understand very well.

Finally, an interpreter said, "Orya now has another wife. She will be willing to take care of Josie."

The missionaries were glad; Josie could return to her own people. So they made arrangements to bring Josie to them in two weeks.

Before leaving, the missionary family was served a delicious meal of sticky pounded yams and peppery chicken gravy. The girls loved to eat *ruam,* because for once they got to use their fingers—no silverware allowed! They were all thankful for the kind hospitality of the Tiv people, who never allow a guest to go away hungry. After eating their fill, the family piled back into their car, laden with gifts of eggs, corn, oranges, and even a scrawny old rooster that crowed all the way home.

Two weeks later, Dianne and the family gathered all of Josie's clothes, milk powder, and lots of bottles of

boiled water. Once more they made the long trip to
Orya's village.

When they arrived at the village, they did not go directly to Orya's compound. Instead, they parked under
a mango tree in a schoolyard nearby. Ever so slowly they
walked the rest of the way down a grassy path to the
compound. The thought of leaving Josie behind tugged
at their hearts. She had lived with the family for six
months, and they would miss her. Besides that, they
now had heard that Orya had a reputation for drinking
and spending the money he earned on gambling. Were
they doing the right thing for Josie? But they had prayed
for wisdom, and God seemed to be guiding them in this
direction.

When they reached the compound, they were again
greeted by a crowd of happy people and they felt a little
better. Josie's parents seemed a little concerned about
how to care for her, but they also seemed very happy
with all the clean, pretty things the missionaries had
brought for the baby.

"This is what she is used to eating," the missionaries
said as they showed the food. "And this is how you mix
the milk. Please boil the drinking water. That will help
her stay healthy."

"We are happy with the food," Orya and his new wife
answered. "It will help us feed Josie. And we thank you
for the things that you brought."

"We have brought you one more present," the missionaries answered. And they gave Orya a Bible written
in the Tiv language. Then they turned to some students
in the crowd. "You can read," they said. "Will you read
this *Bibilo* to Orya?"

"We will," the students promised.

"And I will listen," Josie's father said.

Finally, the missionaries stood to leave. With heavy hearts they said goodbye. Their farewell to Josie was not easy, but they were leaving her in God's care.

The family did see Josie once in a while. They would drive to her village and visit with her family. Although Orya never mentioned the *Bibilo*, they were happy to see that Josie was healthy and growing steadily.

But, when Josie was four years old, the missionary family had to move away from Takum. They would live too far away to visit Josie. So they went for one last visit, but Josie and Orya were not there. They had gone on a journey. Sadly the family went home and packed for their move.

Would they never see Josie again? What would happen to her? Would she grow up hearing God's Word? They had to trust God, they told themselves, even if they never heard of Josie again. But God had a wonderful surprise for them.

One day before the family moved, they heard a knock at their screen door. There stood Josie, holding her father's hand!

"We have heard that you are leaving this area," Orya said. "We have come to say goodbye. And we have come to tell you our wonderful news.

"It is against Tiv custom to take in a strange child and care for it," Orya explained. "But you took in Josie when she needed you. You cared for her and loved her. For many months I thought long and hard about the good things you did for Josie. And I knew you were good people. So I listened when students read the *Bibilo* you gave me. And my family listened. And the *Bibilo* convinced us that we needed Jesus as our Savior. Now my family and I are Christians. We are all attending a Christian church. And we are all praising God!"

The missionary family left Takum with a song in their hearts and praise on their lips. God had answered their prayers for Josie and her family.

"Will you take a baby into your home for a while?" No one knew how important that question was when Nurse Julie first asked it. But God knew. And he used the missionaries' kindness and his Word, the Bible, to bring Josie and her family to him.

The Friend in the Kitchen

"Papa, when are you going to make a fire?"

Many months had passed since the last drops of rain had fallen from the brazen sky. The grass had long since turned a dusty brown. Many thirsty trees had shed their dry, brittle leaves. All the boys in the village knew how very careful they must be with fire. In minutes stray sparks from a careless fire could completely destroy their village of grass-roofed huts.

But Agber and his friends also knew the thrill of huge brush fires. The men in the village started them each year to clear the land for planting. Those fires meant hunting! The heat of the flames forced all sorts of little animals that made their homes in the tall grass to run for their lives. The boys would be ready for them with sticks and machetes. Each boy hoped he would be able to carry home a prize—a plump, giant bush rat for mother to cook for supper!

Agber's father smiled broadly, his white teeth glistening in his dark face. "Soon, my boy. Maybe tomorrow. We have been very busy putting new grass roofs on our huts. When that work is finished, we will be ready to do some hunting."

Life in Agber's village was full. For as long as he could remember, he and his family had shared the small round, mud-bricked hut he called home. He and his friends spent many happy hours playing with crude toys they made from old tin cans, wire, and bamboo sticks.

As soon as he was old enough, Agber had begun to help his father and mother in their farm plot, digging, planting, and weeding with a small, hand-held hoe. He often fetched buckets of water from the water hole for Mother, or carried and chopped firewood for her cooking fire.

He loved the delicious fruit which, when in season, he and his friends could eat until they were full. Mangos were sweet and juicy, oranges quenched their thirst, strawberrylike guavas tasted delicious, and the cashew pears were delightfully sour and puckery.

But Agber's favorite times were nights when the villagers sat leisurely around crackling fires, with the velvety black, star-studded African sky stretched out above them. It was then that the older men began telling stories. Stories about animals always taught a lesson; legends told him of the beginnings of his tribe, the Tiv; riddles sometimes took days to solve; humorous talks with ridiculous things made everyone roll with laughter. Yes, those were Agber's most precious times. Then he felt most of all that he truly belonged, that he was completely happy.

Agber knew too that he was a very privileged boy, for he went to school. Early each morning, while it was still somewhat cool, he and his friends walked to the mission school at Harga. There Agber learned many exciting things about his world. His favorite stories were those about Jesus. It was an important day for the boy when he stood in front of the small church in Harga and was baptized by Missionary Baker. Agber had grown to be a strong young man. He looked ahead eagerly to what God had planned for his life.

Agber's father could not afford to send him to high school. So Agber began working as a cook for a missionary family. He was very bright and quickly caught on to the trick of reading recipes. He soon discovered that he really enjoyed cooking, and that he was good at it. He and the missionaries' children became fast friends. Agber usually had a snack on hand to satisfy hungry appetites: roasted or boiled peanuts, freshly cut pineapple, maybe a just-baked cooky.

Agber married a beautiful young Christian girl. Together they had two little boys of their own. In time Agber and his family moved far away to the large city of Jos. What a change from living in the bush!

But Agber loved his new job. He worked as a cook in Mountain View Hostel. Mountain View was a big home for missionary children. Agber had always missed the missionary children while they were many miles away at boarding school. They came home only twice each year for school vacations. Now he worked at the very place they lived while they attended school. And making the children happy by fixing delicious food for them gave Agber great joy.

Agber soon became a favorite with the missionary children. He fed them and played with them. He teased them and loved them. Each morning as they walked into the big kitchen for breakfast, Agber's cheery grin welcomed them. "'Allo, David! Eh-heh, muy friend, Kim. 'Morning, Jon!" He was always patient with them, always ready to give a helping hand when needed.

As the years passed, many, many missionary children learned to love the friendly, big, black man in the white apron. When they arrived on the first day of school, still crying inside from the pain of leaving parents and little brothers or sisters far away at home, Agber's familiar face welcomed and cheered them. On the last day of school it was always hard to say goodbye to their friend in the kitchen.

One day the children noticed that Agber was missing. "Uncle Jerry, where is Agber?" they asked their housefather.

"He has not been feeling very well lately. I took him to the hospital for some tests," explained Uncle Jerry. "Things do not look very good for him."

As the days passed, Agber's friends watched him grow weaker and thinner. The strapping big man was slowly wasting away. Inside his body a deadly cancer grimly took its toll.

The children missed the jokes and teasing. The cheerful grin they so loved was fading. Agber faithfully worked as long as he had strength. But, one day his strength was finished. He stayed nearby in his small home, sleeping or resting outdoors in the shade. His wife tenderly cared for him. His two sons could not understand what had happened to their strong father. The missionary children quietly walked over to greet their friend each day. Everyone knew it would not be long.

One night the children were awakened by the sound of drums and singing. It came from the direction of Agber's house. They realized that their friend had left them. Agber had left his suffering body for a strong, new life in heaven. The sound they heard was that of Agber's Christian friends. As was their custom, they had come to comfort Agber's family with their singing.

A few days later, Agber's friends laid his body to rest at his home near Harga. They would miss him very much. The kitchen seemed empty without him. The missionary children spoke often of their friend.

Christmas was only a few weeks away when one of the little boys had a happy thought. "Agber is going to have Christmas in heaven, isn't he? He will like that!" Then they realized that, because Agber had loved Jesus, he had been ready to meet him. They would never forget their big friend in the kitchen. He had shown them what Jesus' love really meant.

5

A New Suit for Alu

"*A tese Iyoci*, please come to the dispensary right away. There is a child who just arrived. He is very sick. You must come and see him."

Maryamu, a pleasant young Nigerian nurse, knocked politely at the screen door of Nurse Betty's small round home. She waited patiently for her friend to put on her shoes and find her flashlight. It was late in the evening, the perfect time for snakes to be out hunting their supper. Nurse Betty wanted to avoid any chance of stepping on one.

As they walked quickly to the small collection of mud huts which made up the Kunav dispensary, Maryamu told Nurse Betty about the child. He was a little boy about four years old, she said. He had just arrived with his mother and grandmother. They had traveled many hours to get to the dispensary. First they had gone on foot, mother and grandmother taking turns carrying the little boy, then across a river in a tippy canoe, and finally on the back of a bumpy, dusty truck jammed with sweaty, noisy people. The little boy was very, very sick.

As she stepped into the room, Nurse Betty waited a

few moments for her eyes to adjust to the dim light from a tiny kerosene lantern burning in the center of the hut. She looked around for her little patient. Ah, there he was, lying on the floor near his mother. "Poor little fellow," she thought when she saw that he did not have on a single stitch of clothing. "He must be cold." She gently covered the boy with a clean light blanket. "*Iti nyi* (What is his name)?" she asked.

"Alu," his mother replied sadly. She expected her son to die soon. She had brought him to the mission dispensary only because there was nothing else left to do.

"What is wrong with Alu?" asked Nurse Betty as she quickly examined the child. She noticed that his jaws seemed to be locked tightly together. His face wore an unchanging twisted look of pain.

"He cannot walk. He cannot talk. He cannot eat. I can do nothing for him," explained Alu's mother hopelessly in her own Tiv language.

"First of all," decided Nurse Betty when she saw Alu's thin wasted body, "we must get some food into this child." She asked Maryamu to mix some powdered milk and clean water. Then she gently lifted Alu to a sitting position and carefully forced tiny amounts of milk into his mouth. She had to be very careful that he did not choke.

At first Alu did not seem to like this new taste. The only milk he had tasted was his mother's milk, when he was a baby. But gradually he got used to it and stopped fighting every spoonful. When Nurse Betty felt that he had taken enough milk, she laid Alu down again.

"Please bring some warm water in a bowl," she told Maryamu. Then she carefully washed the dirty little body and tried to make Alu as comfortable as possible.

Knowing they had done all they could that evening,

Nurse Betty explained to Alu's mother and grandmother how she would be caring for Alu, and what they must do to help. She finished with a quiet prayer in the Tiv language so that Alu's family would know that it was God alone who would be able to heal the little boy. They needed his help desperately. Nurse Betty did not have the heart to tell them that she did not think Alu would get better. He was a very, very sick little boy.

The days and nights that followed were long for Alu's mother and grandmother. They took turns sleeping and watching their little boy. They did their best to feed him and keep him warm and clean as Nurse Betty had instructed them. They watched with great interest as nurses gave him shots and took his temperature. Little Alu could not talk, but his big brown eyes slowly seemed to brighten and respond to all the attention and care he was getting.

One day Nurse Betty stopped by to visit her little patient. "*M'sugh*, Alu," she greeted the child. Lifting him carefully onto her lap, she prayed with him. "Please, *Yesu*, make Alu all better so he can walk and talk like other children." Then she took his little black face between her hands and said, "Alu, when you can walk again, I want you to walk to my house. It is not very far from here. At my house I have a nice white suit for you. It will be yours to wear. And I will bake a loaf of bread for you. It will be yours to take home with you."

Alu looked unbelievingly into his white friend's eyes. Then ever so slowly, for the first time, his little face broke into a crooked smile. With happy tears Nurse Betty, Mother, and Grandmother thanked God for this moment, the moment for which they all had been waiting and praying.

Five days later, Nurse Betty was enjoying a cup of tea

on her veranda (porch) when she noticed a little procession slowly approaching. What was this, another emergency? But as they came nearer, she recognized Alu's mother, his grandmother, and smiling broadly, surrounded by a group of new friends from the dispensary, little Alu.

Step . . . step . . . step . . . step. Walking was still difficult for Alu. He could not bend his knees yet. He walked as if he were on stilts. But he walked!

When the procession reached her house, Nurse Betty picked up Alu and hugged him joyfully. Then she told everyone to wait, they would be back. Taking Alu into her house, she dressed him in the little white shorts and shirt she had promised. She slipped bright blue little thongs onto his feet. Then she carried him into her pantry and gave him a loaf of bread neatly tied in a plastic bag. Triumphantly they returned to Alu's waiting friends. Amid cheers and clapping, Alu was returned to his proud mother's arms. Before they left, Nurse Betty led them in a prayer of thanks to God for making Alu so much better.

A week later, Alu's mother and grandmother begged Nurse Betty to allow them to return to their village. Alu could speak a few words now. He had begun to swallow liquids much more easily. He missed his own home very much and longed to go back to it.

Alu really should have stayed a bit longer, but Nurse Betty knew he would be all right. He was still very weak, so she arranged for them to travel with some friends of hers. Then, reluctantly, she hugged her little friend goodbye. Alu smiled and waved until he could no longer see his white friend.

Nurse Betty turned slowly toward the dispensary. Her heart was filled with praise to God. Not only had he made Alu well again, he had also made it possible for Alu, his mother, and his grandmother to hear the wonderful news that Jesus loved them. Nurse Betty knew they would not forget what they had seen and heard in the weeks of Alu's illness. She knew that the tiny seed of God's Word had surely been planted in their hearts. She felt like singing and shouting for joy, "Thank you, God!"

And then Maryamu met her with a report on a new patient.

Stuck in the Stream

"Come on, girls," said Mother. "Let's try to finish this packing before dinnertime."

"I sure wish the summer had not gone so fast," remarked Ann. "It seems like we just came home, and already it's time to leave again."

"I dread having to think about homework again," Rose added. "I wonder who will be in my room in the dorm this term."

"You'll know tomorrow," Mother replied. "Tomorrow will be here soon enough."

And it was. After an early breakfast, it was time to load the waiting car with all sorts of bags and suitcases. Amazingly, everything fit in. The small group of parents and children prayed together for safety on the long journey ahead. Then the most difficult moment came, the time to say goodbye. Everyone had trouble holding back the tears.

"Bye, Dad and Mom. I sure love you!"

"Thanks for everything. I'm going to miss you so much!"

"Goodbye, Sweetheart. We hope to see you in two months."

The children finally piled into the car. Then they were off, waving their arms, pressing their tear-stained faces to the window and trying hard to be brave.

Some missionary children in Nigeria pack suitcases instead of lunchpails. And they fly to school in airplanes instead of riding in schoolbuses. That may be fun, but they do not get to come home every afternoon after school. Instead, they live at school and do not see their families for many weeks at a time.

When this story took place, the children were not able to fly to school as usual. Instead, they had to make the long journey by road. In those days, the roads in Nigeria were very rough and bumpy. They were not the smooth paved freeways that we have in North America. It would take many hours, perhaps most of the day, to cover the three hundred miles to school.

Two dads, whom the children called Uncle Harold and Uncle Herm, shared the driving. The children passed the time by singing and telling jokes and stories. Then they began to make plans for lunch.

"Why don't we eat by Assob Falls?" suggested Judy. "There's a nice picnic spot there." Everyone readily agreed. They should be that far by lunch time if everything went well.

They had been riding several hours when the men decided to take a different road they had heard about, a shortcut. After all, the main road was already so bad, a shortcut couldn't be much worse, could it? It didn't take long to discover that a shortcut could be worse, much worse!

Not a single stream had a bridge over it, so they rode through stream after stream. Everyone in the car was thankful that the water was not very high and the streams were not very wide.

Finally, they decided to stop in a village and ask how much farther it was to the main road. A Nigerian man answered them, "One more big stream. No bridge. Remain two miles." It was too late to turn back, so on they bumped. Rounding a curve, they stopped on a high ridge that overlooked the last large stream.

"Wow!" breathed Rose in a small voice. "How are we ever going to get across *that*?"

"All right, children, you get out while we look things over," Uncle Harold instructed.

The men carefully waded down into the water, trying to decide on the safest route. Then very slowly they drove down the steep bank and into the water while the children watched from above. Suddenly, halfway through the stream, the car jerked to a halt. It would not move another inch. A hidden log, which had once been part of a bridge, had caught the rear axle. The men tried everything they could think of to pry the log loose, but nothing worked. Not even the crowd of curious Nigerians who had appeared out of nowhere could push or pull the car free.

Finally, Uncle Herm said that he would walk two miles to the main road and look for help. The men carried the children piggyback across the stream to where they could pass the time exploring.

Suddenly, thunder rumbled in the distance. The sky turned dark; a tropical storm was coming.

"Is it going to rain?" one of the smallest girls asked fearfully. "I'm afraid of thunder. I wish my mommy was here." And she started to cry.

"Let's get back into the car to stay dry," called Uncle Harold. All the children hurried to obey. By the time the first drops fell, they had all been safely carried back to the car.

"How about a picnic?" suggested Uncle Harold brightly. No one was really very hungry, but they got out their sandwiches anyway. Before they ate, they bowed their heads together. "Dear Lord," Uncle Harold prayed, "please help us get out of this stream. May Uncle Herm find help for us at the main road. And thank you for our lunch. Amen."

As they sat quietly trying to enjoy their food, an older girl started chuckling. "This is different," she said. "We planned to eat *by* a waterfall, not *in* a stream!" The smiles helped ease the tension a little. They would have a good story to tell back at school, if they ever got there.

Uncle Harold had just opened the car door another time to check the rising water when somebody shouted, "Listen! Something is coming!"

Sure enough. "Putt-putt-putt-putt." Everyone heard it. They all glued their eyes to the curve in the road ahead. What do you suppose came into view? A tractor! And Uncle Herm was sitting up with the driver, waving triumphantly.

Now, you may not think it so special to find a tractor. But every one of those children knew that a tractor was very rare in Nigeria. This was perhaps the only one within hundreds of miles! Yet God had planned for it to be on the main road at the very moment Uncle Herm arrived there for help.

In no time at all the men fastened a heavy chain to the car, around a tree and onto the tractor. Amid cheers and shouts of joy the tractor slowly pulled the car loose and out onto dry land.

They were bouncing along again when a small voice piped up. "Shouldn't we have another prayer meeting and thank God for getting us out of the stream?" Right there they stopped and bowed their heads to thank God for his wonderful care.

The next day, on their way home, Uncle Harold and Uncle Herm drove back to the stream, just to see how it was. Imagine their amazement when they found that it had become a raging torrent, swollen far beyond its banks. As they turned toward home, their hearts were again filled with praise and thankfulness to God for hearing their prayers and caring for them so wonderfully.

The Prisoner

Dza-yol sat on the hard bench in her dark, smelly prison cell, wiping away tears that just kept flowing. Being in prison was awful. The judge had not cared about her tears and did not even listen when she said, "I didn't mean to do it!" But something worse was coming; she was going to die!

"You did it," the judge had said. "You killed your husband's other wife, and you must die. You must be hanged."

Hanged! What an awful thing! A rope around her neck. Dza-yol shuddered at the thought. She didn't want to die! She was afraid to die. She covered her face with her hands and sobbed. Was there no way out? Her husband didn't care at all. The judge didn't listen. She had appealed to the governor, but he wouldn't listen, either. What could she do?

She stopped sobbing and began to think. Carefully she reviewed everything that had happened.

Her husband, Agera, had been a good husband, and she had tried to be a good wife. She had been happy fetching water for him, tending the garden, and cooking his meals. The men of the compound often praised her

yams because she pounded them hard and they were
not lumpy. They also praised the peppery gravy that she
made from bush rats, duiker, bush cow, or whatever Agera
brought home from hunting. There was always plenty
to eat, and Dza-yol knew how to make the food taste
good.

But one day Agera told her that he was going away to
look for a new wife. Dza-yol remembered how shocked
she was when she heard that. "Why do you want another
wife?" she asked. "Have I not been a good wife? Have
I not served you well these many years?"

Agera had tried to make her feel better. He said that
she would be first wife; the second wife would have to
do whatever Dza-yol told her to do. But that did not
help at all; Dza-yol did not want Agera to get another
wife.

Yet Agera went away and found another wife. In fact,
he had to borrow money to buy just the woman he
wanted. Then he returned with his new wife and many
of her friends. They were all singing, dancing and
celebrating.

Dza-yol couldn't forget how hard she had tried to join
the people of the compound shouting, "*Melaba! Melaba*
(Welcome! Welcome)!" But her heart wasn't in it. How
could she welcome another wife? Deep down inside,
Dza-yol already hated that other woman.

Weeks passed. Dza-yol tried to be faithful in her work.
She told the new wife, Nguwan, what to do and how to
please Agera. Dza-yol tried to be a good wife, but she
was hurt. She could see that Agera favored Nguwan and
was much kinder to her than he was to Dza-yol.

One day Nguwan called to Dza-yol, "Come here!
Come to my hut!" Dza-yol went to the hut, and Nguwan
shouted at her, "What did you do with my money?"

"What money?" Dza-yol asked. "I did not take any of your money. I don't need your money!"

"My money from selling rice!" Nguwan shouted. "It was right here in my basket, and now it's gone!" She turned her little basket upside down and shook it. "See? It's gone! You took it! Go get it and bring it back!"

Dza-yol shouted back at her, "I did not take your money! How dare you call me a liar?"

Agera came to see what the shouting was all about. He made both women keep still.

"Dza-yol!"

"Yes?"

"What has happened?"

"She says I took her money."

"She *did* take my money!" Nguwan shouted.

"Nguwan!"

"Yes?"

"How much money was taken?"

"All of it! Eight shillings! I got it by selling rice."

"Dza-yol, give her the money. Immediately!"

"But I did not take it!"

"You must have taken it. It's gone. Who else could have taken it? Now go get it!"

Dza-yol remembered how terrible she felt. Her husband would not believe her. He had called her a liar. She remembered stumbling, heart seething with anger and hurt, toward her own hut. She did not have the money; what could she do?

Then the awful thing happened. As she reached the door of her hut, Dza-yol heard footsteps behind her. She turned and saw Nguwan, her face twisted with anger and hatred. Sunlight flashed on a knife that Nguwan held high. Frightened by the knife, Dza-yol hit Nguwan's arm. The knife fell, and Dza-yol quickly snatched it up. She turned to hurry into her hut. But Nguwan took a wooden pestle and hit Dza-yol's head, hard. Angrily, Dza-yol turned around, swinging the knife wildly. She hit Nguwan. Nguwan fell to the ground, bleeding, with the knife still in her. Minutes later Nguwan was dead.

Sitting on the little prison bench, remembering it all, Dza-yol covered her face with her hands and began to wail again. "I didn't mean to do that! I didn't mean to!" But she had done it. She had killed her husband's second wife!

She could not forget Agera's angry words. "You have killed her! You are an evil woman!"

The police had come and taken her to prison. The judge had decided that she must die as punishment. She would be hanged!

Suddenly Dza-yol remembered something and stopped wailing. Wasn't there a missionary near her village? Everybody said that he was a good man who wanted to help people. Maybe he could help her! The next time a guard came, Dza-yol asked him to please go find the missionary.

Dza-yol jumped up from her stool when the guard brought Mr. Terpstra, the missionary. Excitedly, she began to tell her story. She talked very quickly, and she spoke Hausa, a language Mr. Terpstra didn't yet understand very well. But he listened carefully. He prayed that God would help him understand so that he could help.

The misssionary took Dza-yol back to the judge. This time, when Dza-yol told her story in Hausa, Mr. Terpstra translated it into English. The judge didn't understand Hausa at all. When the judge heard the story in English, he understood. He knew then that fear and anger had made Dza-yol stab wildly. He realized that she hadn't meant to kill Nguwan.

"You do not deserve to die," the judge said to Dza-yol. "Instead, you must stay in prison for ten years."

How happy Dza-yol was!

Back in the prison cell, the missionary told Dza-yol about Jesus who died so that all our sins could be forgiven. Dza-yol knew that she had sinned; she had hated Nguwan and she had been very angry. She confessed her sins and became a Christian.

The ten years in prison went fast for Dza-yol. She was a happy Christian because she knew God had forgiven her sins. When another prisoner beat her with a stick, Dza-yol didn't turn back in anger. Instead, she told that prisoner about the love of Jesus.

After ten years, Dza-yol was set free. She left the prison for a short time. Soon she returned, but not as a prisoner. She became a helper there. Dza-yol the Christian spent many hours telling the prisoners about the love of God and about Jesus. And often she told her special story about how God had saved her and made her truly happy.

8

A Surprise from God

*Before they call I will answer; while they
are still speaking I will hear.* Isaiah 65:24

"You may go home tomorrow, Ma-gen," the doctor
said. "You have improved a lot since your operation, and
you seem to be feeling much better. If you take care of
yourself, you may go tomorrow morning."

Ma-gen smiled at the doctor from her hospital bed.
"Thank you," she whispered. She closed her eyes as the
doctor left the room and lost herself in thought.

Less than a week before, she had stumbled into this
mission hospital, very ill and very fearful. She had walked
nine miles from her home and could scarcely drag herself into Mkar, the town where the hospital stood. All
the way she had worried and wondered. She was not a
Christian; would the people at a mission hospital help
her? What was wrong with her? Would they care?

Now she knew. The doctors and nurses had taken her
in immediately and given her loving care. They had discovered what was wrong and had helped her with an
operation. And throughout her stay here they had talked
about—and they had shown—the love of Jesus.

47

"This is a good hospital," Ma-gen thought, "with good people. But I will be glad to go home tomorrow. Now that I am better, I'll enjoy the walk." And she fell asleep.

The sun rose early the next morning. A cool breeze blew through the hospital window and the birds sang outside. It was a beautiful day to walk home. Ma-gen wrapped her few things in a bundle and left the hospital, eager to be on her way.

Just about the time Ma-gen left the hospital, a missionary left his home and went to his office. Peter Bulthuis had work to do. A cool breeze blew through his office window and he heard the birds sing outside as he sorted papers and letters.

But he didn't work long. He felt restless and couldn't keep his mind on what he was doing. He didn't know why he couldn't work. He tried to forget his restless feeling, but he couldn't. "Maybe if I work in my garden I'll get over this strange feeling," he told himself. So he locked up his office and went home.

Meanwhile, Ma-gen had begun to walk more slowly on her trek home. The cool breeze had died down, and the sun shone hot. She felt weak from her stay in the hospital and found that she tired very easily. She had to stop and rest again and again.

After walking about a mile, Ma-gen was simply too tired to go on. Alongside the road someone had plowed a field and heaped the soil into mounds for planting yams. Ma-gen put her little bundle on the ground and sat down on one of those mounds. It was better than sitting on the hard ground. She was so very, very tired, she did not know what to do next. She knew she could not walk the rest of the way home.

Back in his garden, Mr. Bulthuis began working hard, hoeing his tomato patch. But the hard work didn't help one bit. The strange feeling would not go away. He brought the hoe back to the tool shed. Now what?

He got into his car and started down the road. He turned onto the rough dirt road that led to the village of Gboko. He didn't know why he went that way; that was always such a bumpy road. A little way ahead, he saw a woman sitting on a yam heap.

Meanwhile, Ma-gen, sitting on the yam heap, tried to think what she should do. How could she get home? She knew of only one man who had a car—Bohii. If only he would come and take her home!

Then she remembered what the Christians had told her: she could pray and God would hear her prayer. But she wasn't a Christian! Would he hear her prayer? She certainly needed help!

Finally, Ma-gen did what she had seen the Christians do; she bowed her head and closed her eyes. Then she prayed, "God, send Bohii with his car." And when she opened her eyes, there he was!

Ma-gen jumped up and shouted, "He heard me! He heard me! And I'm not yet a Christian!"

Mr. Bulthuis stopped his car, thinking maybe the woman needed help. When he heard what she said he understood his strange feelings. God had sent him here!

Ma-gen picked up her bundle and hobbled to the car. Mr. Bulthuis helped her get in. As they rode along, Ma-gen told how she had prayed and what a wonderful surprise it was to see Bohii there when she opened her eyes. Then she asked, "How did God tell you that I needed you?"

Mr. Bulthuis told her how God had made him restless and even led him to get into his car and drive down the right road. He tried to explain how God began to answer her prayer long before Ma-gen had prayed, so that he was there when she finished praying.

When they came to her village, he said, "Tell your people to gather tomorrow morning and I will come. We will have a church service together."

The next morning a crowd was waiting for Mr. Bulthuis when he arrived. Everyone was excited. "God answered Ma-gen's prayer," they said, "and she wasn't even a Christian yet."

They listened quietly to the story of Hannah, who prayed for a child. When they heard "God can answer prayer today, too," they all said, "Yes! He answered Ma-gen's prayer yesterday!"

Ma-gen became a strong Christian. Many others from her village also believed and were baptized. Soon there was a church in Ma-gen's village.

God doesn't answer all prayers in such a surprising way. Sometimes he lets us wait a long time for an answer, and sometimes the answer is no. He answered Ma-gen's prayer so that she could tell other people how great and wonderful he is. And Ma-gen's story proves that God does hear us. Sometimes he begins to answer even before we ask him.

A Time for War

"**H**urry, Ojuku, hurry! We must run or they will kill us!" Mama clasped Baby Ruth tightly to her. With the other hand she pulled Ojuku along beside her. It was dark. The little fellow could hardly see where they were going.

Ojuku's thoughts rushed from one thing to another. Why wasn't Mama using the street as she usually did? Why were they running from one dark place to another? This seemed like a game of hide-and-seek. He and his friends used to love hiding among the rocks and trees behind their apartment home. Their games were usually about soldiers. There were many soldiers around these days. His father was a soldier. Ojuku and Mama had said goodbye to him several weeks earlier. Ojuku had been proud of Father in his smart green uniform, his big black boots, and his dangerous gun. Many of the other boys in Ojuku's neighborhood had soldier fathers, too. Ojuku wondered what his friends were doing. He wished his best buddy, Ebe, was with him now. That would help make the knot of fear in his stomach go away. Ebe could always make a good joke out of anything.

"Mama, where are we going?" panted Ojuku. His short legs were becoming very tired.

"Shhhh," whispered Mama, stopping briefly to move Baby Ruth to her other arm. "Just follow me, Ojuku, and be very quiet. I will explain it all to you later, when we are safe." And on they went, down narrow alleys, behind dark buildings, running, walking, stopping to catch their breath, and running on again.

At last Mama pointed to a row of bright spotlights ahead. "Look over there, Ojuku. That is the police station. When we get there we will be safe. Can you run a little farther?"

Ojuku blinked his eyes as they stepped out of the darkness into a brightly lit yard crowded with people. Everywhere he looked he saw policemen with guns. The noise of people shouting, talking, weeping and moaning confused Ojuku. Baby Ruth began to cry.

"Quickly! In through the gate!" barked a tall black policeman. Mama held tightly to Ojuku's hand so they would not become separated in the crowd.

"Attention, please! Attention!" boomed another voice on a loudspeaker. "You are all safe here. We will protect you from any who wish to kill you. The walls are strong. We have many policemen with guns. We are making arrangements to transport all of you back to the East as soon as possible."

"Where is the East, Mama?" whispered Ojuku. "I don't want to go anywhere else. I want to go home."

"Shhhh," comforted Mama as she put her arm around the trembling little fellow. "There is a war in our country. Some of the tribes are fighting each other. We are Ibos. We come from the eastern part of Nigeria. The people here in the North do not want us to stay. Tonight there is much killing in this city. We had to come here for protection. Listen! Can you hear the guns?"

As Ojuku listened his eyes became big and round.

Yes, he did hear them. "Are bad men killing our people?" he asked fearfully.

"Yes, Ojuku, but God can keep us safe," replied Mama. "Now try to go to sleep. We will see what tomorrow brings."

Ojuku curled up in the dirt, his head on his mother's lap. Oh, how he wished Father was here. What was going to happen to their home? To his friends? To him?

Bright sunlight shone into Ojuku's eyes and wakened him the next morning. At first he did not know where he was. And then it all came rushing back—the frightening run in the middle of the night, the bright lights, the big policemen with guns. "Mama!" he cried out fearfully.

"I am right here, son."

"Mama, I am hungry."

"Here is a banana for you, Ojuku. Eat it slowly, because I do not have more. I did not have time to take any more food along last night."

As Ojuku sat slowly eating his banana breakfast, he began to take a careful look around him. "What a lot of people," he thought to himself. "It is so full in here, I can hardly move!"

Suddenly he caught sight of a familiar face. "Ebe!" he shouted joyfully to his friend and waved his banana peeling. Ebe, too, was overjoyed to see Ojuku, and the two boys were soon discussing the latest events with great excitement.

"Shall we take a look around?" suggested Ebe.

"Better ask our mamas first," advised Ojuku.

Ojuku's mother smiled. "Yes, you may," she replied. "I doubt that you could get lost here if you tried."

Ojuku was startled to see how sad and tired Mama

looked. He must remember to take good care of her, he thought. He had promised Father that he would.

The two boys slowly made their way toward the main gate. Something interesting seemed to be going on there, but they could not see what it was. There were too many people in the way.

"My mama said there is a war," announced Ojuku.

"Yeah. And my mama said we are lucky to be alive," added Ebe. "She said. . . ."

"Oh! Look, Ebe! Ebe, look!" Ojuku grabbed his friend by the arm and stood as if rooted to the ground. There before them, under a large open shelter in the corner of the police yard, lay all sorts of sick and wounded people. Lying on mats on the ground, many of them were covered with blood and dirt and grass.

As the boys watched, a group of white people entered the gate. Several of them carried huge kettles, bowls and spoons. Ojuku saw that some of them wore white uniforms. He knew that they were doctors and nurses.

After a brief prayer and a few instructions, the white people walked over to the shelter and began dishing steaming hot porridge into the bowls. Many of those people looked like teen-agers.

"They are big missionary children from the boarding school in Jos," whispered Ebe. Ojuku wondered how his friend always seemed to know so much about everything.

The boys watched with fascination as the missionaries quickly scattered throughout the sick shelter. One carefully lifted a weak old man and spooned porridge into his mouth. Another gave a new young mother a bowl of nourishing food while one of the white girls held her newborn baby. They washed and bandaged cuts and wounds. They gave shots and spooned medicine into patients too weak to sit up alone. Ojuku closed his eyes quickly to block out a sight he knew only too well. A doctor and nurse were carefully covering a person for whom help had come too late, another dead one.

Twice each day the two boys watched the missionaries come with food and loving care. The boys knew now that none of their own Nigerian people dared to help the refugees. When there is war, nobody trusts anyone.

One day, the voice on the loudspeaker made another announcement. "Attention please! Attention! Tomorrow you will all be leaving for the East. There will be many trucks to take you. Police will go along to protect you from enemies on the way. Anyone who is too sick to make the journey by road will be flown by airplane. All Ibos must leave."

The missionaries came for the last time. They said goodbye to many new friends. "We will be praying for you," they said. "May God bring you safely to the East. And may he someday bring you back here to your homes."

Ojuku clung tightly to Mama's hand as they stood waiting to board the big truck that would take them far away. He knew why Mama had tears in her eyes. They were taking nothing with them. They had left everything in their house that dark frightening night when they had run for their lives. Mama's pretty dishes, their new Christmas clothes, the book with Ojuku's baby pictures, their precious Ibo Bible, everything had to stay behind.

Ojuku didn't know that they would never see their things again. Already their home had been wrecked and ruined by enemies who hated his people, the Ibos. His baby pictures lay crumpled on the floor. The pages ripped out of the Bible blew sadly in the breeze. Mama's dishes lay smashed on a heap of rubbish. It was a good thing Ojuku did not know that.

Ojuku and Ebe made sure their mamas kept together so that they would be on the same truck. The whole thing seemed a great adventure to the two boys. The line of noisy diesel-smelling trucks kept coming and coming. People would fill a truck, and an empty one would take its place. The boys thought it would never end.

At last it was their turn. A tall policeman boosted Ojuku up high. He quickly sat down on the hard wooden bench next to Mama and Baby Ruth. He wanted to make sure he had a place before someone else sat in it.

The long, long row of trucks, jam-packed with people made quite a sight as it moved out of the city. Although Ojuku and Ebe did not know it, many of the missionaries were watching from their windows.

"Goodbye! Goodbye!" They waved at the endless line of black faces passing by. "May God keep you safe." They felt almost as if a part of them was leaving, too.

"Look! An airplane!" Ebe poked Ojuku, who had fallen asleep in the hot sun. The boys were growing very tired from many hours of riding on the dusty bumpy road. They were thirsty and hungry. When were they going to reach Makurdi? Mama had said it would take all day, but would the day never end? Ojuku was glad for a bit of excitement.

The boys watched with great interest as the small airplane swooped down over them and then disappeared into the distance. It did this several times throughout the day. "That is the airplane of the mission," said Ebe's mother. "I think it is checking on us."

"Did you see the white man back there?" asked Ojuku's mother. "I know him. He is missionary Dean.

He is coming along with us in case we need any help along the way."

It was very dark when they drew up near the city of Makurdi. Before them lay a wide river. Over the river was a bridge wide enough for one truck. On the bridge and on each side were many soldiers with guns.

The soldiers could decide to kill all the hated Ibos. Or they could refuse to let them cross the bridge. Or they could give their permission to continue the journey to the East. A missionary from Makurdi had to get permission from the soldiers for all the trucks to cross the bridge safely.

Missionary DeGroot had been waiting at the bridge. The mission's airplane pilot had told him when to expect the trucks to arrive there. Now he got out of his car and walked slowly toward a group of soldiers guarding the bridge. With a prayer in his heart he walked up to a soldier. "Good evening," he said politely.

As the soldier turned, Missionary DeGroot could smell that he had been drinking. "What do you want?" snarled the soldier. He jammed his gun against the missionary's chest, his finger on the trigger.

The missionary knew he was in God's hands. Very politely and quietly he explained his request, all the while praying for God's protection.

The soldier glared at him. Then suddenly it seemed that an unseen hand slowly moved the gun away. An officer appeared, gave his permission, and soon the long line of trucks began moving slowly across the darkened bridge.

Ojuku and Ebe looked sleepily at the lights of the city they were entering. They were so tired. They wanted to get out and stretch and run and sleep.

"We will be stopping very soon," promised Mama.

"This is as far as the trucks will take us. I do not know how we will go the rest of the way."

"Maybe on a train," suggested Ojuku hopefully. He had noticed that they had just crossed train tracks. He had always wanted to ride on a train.

"No, I'm afraid not, son," replied Mama. "Because of the war, the trains are not running now. But do not worry. God will take care of us."

At last the trucks stopped. The passengers were unloaded into a large field surrounded by barbed wire. There were many more policemen with guns guarding them. "It's like we are prisoners," complained Ebe.

"No, son," corrected his mother. "It is to keep us safe."

Not far away, Missionary DeGroot, his wife, and Missionary Dean were having a midnight prayer meeting. They were asking God to help them find a way to get all the Ibo people who had come on the trucks back to their homeland in the East. No one dared to drive into the war zone. And the trains had stopped running weeks ago. But wait! What was that?

"Toooot!" A shrill train whistle pierced the silent blackness of the night. But the trains weren't running now.

"Toooot!" Yes, it *was* a train! From out of nowhere, it seemed, a huge black steam engine hissed and wheezed to a stop nearby. Behind it rolled a long line of empty train cars.

The missionaries thanked and praised God as they rushed to help load the hundreds of refugees onto the mysterious train. Ojuku and Ebe could hardly stand the excitement. They would have a real train ride after all!

As the train pulled slowly out of the station, cheers

of joy mixed with tears and prayers of gratitude. In only a few hours they would be back in the East.

The months ahead would be very difficult. Thousands of children would starve to death. The war would take many more lives. Yet Ojuku and Ebe and their families knew they were safe. They belonged to God and he would take care of them, no matter what happened.

10

Lydia

Lydia was gathering sticks for Mother's cooking fire when she heard the sound. She stopped and listened. Was it a "motah"? Not many "motahs" came to the little African village of Nyankwala. The road was rough hard ruts in dry weather. During the rainy season it was sticky, gooey mud. Some days not even one car came! But once a month the missionary came from Wukari. Maybe this was the missionary's "motah" she heard. She laid her handful of sticks on the ground and ran toward her little round mud-brick home.

"Mama! Mama! I hear a motah! I think the missionary is coming!"

A tall black lady in a neat, colorful cloth wrapper came to the door. Lydia's two little sisters peeked from behind their mama's skirt. They all stood quietly and listened. Sure enough, they heard a "motah." Soon the missionary's car came bouncing along and stopped right in front of the house.

Mrs. Boer stepped out of the car and came toward them, smiling broadly. Mr. Boer came around from the other side of the car. Mama called Lydia's daddy, and they all shook hands, very happy to see each other. Then

60

the adults sat together in the shade on the ground, talking to each other.

Mr. Boer and Lydia's daddy did most of the talking. Daddy was an evangelist. He told the story of Jesus to the village people. Mr. Boer came once a month to see how he was getting along. Most of their talk was about Daddy's work.

Lydia didn't listen very long. She went back to work, picking up sticks. While she worked, she kept thinking how nice it would be to go home with the missionaries. She would like to live with them for a while. The more she thought about it, the more she wanted to go.

After a while Lydia saw the missionaries get up to go home. Quickly she ran to her mother. Her big dark eyes sparkled with excitement. "Mama," she said, "I want to follow them!"

Mother looked at her in surprise. Then she said to Mrs. Boer, "Lydia wants to go with you."

"You would have to stay a whole month!" Mrs. Boer replied. "We cannot bring you home if you get homesick. You are only seven years old. You will probably miss your home."

"But I want to go," Lydia insisted. "I won't become homesick. Please, may I go with you?"

Finally both Mother and Mrs. Boer agreed. Lydia could go. So she ran to the "motah" and hopped in, just as she was. She had only her little short skirt and sandals. Her mother did not get a suitcase or pack other clothes for her, because Lydia did not have anything else to wear.

It was thirty miles to Wukari, where the Boers lived. Lydia had never been so far from home! And everything at the missionaries' house was different. Lydia was used to a hard, dry mud floor; the missionaries had little rugs on their floors. Lydia thought that felt good under her bare feet. She had never slept on a bed, but Mrs. Boer made her comfortable on a cot. The food was different, too, but Lydia liked it. Strangest of all, Lydia thought, was the language they spoke. Lydia could not understand English, and the Boers did not speak her language, Jukun, very well. But soon they all learned to speak Hausa together.

Mrs. Boer took Lydia to a store one day and bought material to make her a pretty new dress. Lydia liked that very much. But Mrs. Boer also took her to a doctor, and that frightened Lydia at first. Like many African children, Lydia had never seen a doctor. In fact, many African children become ill, and many die because there are not enough doctors. But Lydia grew and became healthy and strong.

Lydia soon became like a daughter to the Boers, who had no children. They loved her, and she was very happy at their home. The month that she stayed there seemed to fly past.

Soon it was time to return to her village, Nyahkawala. Lydia was glad to see her family again. She ran into her house, quickly changed to her old short skirt, and then played with her brother and sisters just as she used to. There was so much to tell them!

Soon she saw the Boers get up to go home. She ran into her house, changed her clothes again, and came out wearing her new dress. Then she hopped right into the missionaries' car. She wanted to go back with them!

From that time on, the Boers' home was Lydia's home. She returned to Nyahkawala to see her real mother and father once a month. The rest of the time she lived at the missionaries' house.

Lydia loved living with the Boers. She and Mrs. Boer often sang together as they worked. If someone asked

her whose daughter she was, she said, "Mrs. Boer's."
And if the person said, "But that cannot be; they are
white and you are black!" she would say, "God can do
anything!"

One day when the Boers were in Nyahkawala, they
said to Lydia's father, "We would like to send Lydia to
school. She should learn to read and write."

"To school?" her father asked, surprised. "Why should
a girl go to school? Girls do not have to learn to read
and write. They can do their work just as well without
that."

But after they talked it over, he finally agreed. Lydia
would go to school.

Lydia went to the House of Dekker School in Wukari
while she lived with the Boers. She learned very quickly
and enjoyed school tremendously.

Soon it was time for the Boers to go back to the United
States for a vacation furlough. What could Lydia do? She
wanted to keep going to school. The Boers found another family in Wukari with whom Lydia could live
while they were gone. So Lydia still lived in Wukari and
stayed in school, although her new "parents" left for a
while.

Soon after the Boers returned, God gave them a baby
of their own. Lydia loved her new "brother." He was so
different from her, with his pink skin, blue eyes, and
straight yellow hair. And when God gave the Boers a
baby girl, Lydia was happier still. She loved to run her
fingers through her "sister's" silky hair, and then feel
her own tight curls.

At times Mrs. Boer would ask Lydia, "Why did you
want to leave your home and your own father and mother
to come and live with us?"

Lydia would answer, "I don't know. I just wanted to. Something inside of me wanted to."

Now Lydia has a different answer. She knows what that "something inside of her" was.

You see, this all happened years ago. Since then, Lydia has graduated from the House of Dekker School and from high school. All through those years she heard about Jesus, and she learned to love Jesus and wanted to live for him. She met a young man who also loved Jesus. They were married, and today they live in an African village and work for Campus Crusade for Christ. They bring the news of Jesus to other Africans.

At times people still ask Lydia, "Why did you want to leave your home and your own father and mother to go and live with the Boers?"

Now she answers, "God's Spirit spoke to my heart and made me want to go. God helped me grow strong and well and God sent me to school. God's Spirit was getting me ready to work for him!"

11

Snakes, Ants, and Fire

Isn't it wonderful how God takes good care of his children all over this big, beautiful world? No matter what color their skin, no matter what kind of clothes they wear, no matter what language they speak, or where they live, God loves each of his children.

The children in these three short stories used to live in Nigeria, where their father and mother were missionaries. In a way, they are really one story, because they all tell the same thing: God *does* watch over his children.

Little Timmy was only one year old. Children of that age are very curious. They are always getting into some kind of mischief. They want to learn everything they can about the big, exciting world, and so they try to touch and taste everything in their path.

That's how it was with Timmy. He had just learned to walk and was happily playing on the shady big veranda of their house. Suddenly he spied something lying in the warm sunshine on the top step. It looked very interesting indeed! It was long and green, about as big around as his dad's thumb. Timmy toddled toward it to take a closer look. He didn't know that the long green thing was a very poisonous snake.

Timmy was almost close enough to reach out and grab the snake, when Mother happened to look through the screen door to check on him. What she saw nearly made her heart stop. Doing her best to keep calm, she said firmly but quietly, so as not to frighten the snake, "Timmy! No! Come to Mama!"

The little fellow turned his head and then came toddling toward Mother as fast as his chubby legs could carry him, a big grin on his little face, not in the least bit concerned about his narrow escape. Mother picked him up, hugging him tightly to her heart.

Was it just a coincidence that Mother looked out the door at that very moment? Did Timmy always listen to Mother right away, the first time she told him something? No, most little boys and girls need to be told several times to do something. But God was right there with Timmy, taking care that nothing hurt his precious little one.

Then there's the story about the ants.

"There's another one. Quick, step on it!" Those annoying ants seemed to be everywhere—in the sugar, on the floor, in cupboards, even in the Sunday peppermints in Mother's purse! It sometimes helps to set things in water, or to keep them in tightly covered containers. Most ants in Nigeria are simply a big nuisance, but they can give you a good pinch.

However, the dreaded army ants are quite a different story. Traveling in huge bands, they cover anything in their path, even trees and buildings. They usually prey on insects, but they have been known to kill sick or tied-up animals, and even human babies.

It was the middle of the night. The family was peacefully sleeping under their tentlike mosquito nets. Outside, it was pitch dark. There was no electricity in

Nigerian houses in those days, only kerosene or gas lamps, which for the sake of safety from fire were put out at bedtime.

In their room on the corner of the house, Marjo and Marilee began to stir in their sleep. Something was biting them! Waking up, Marilee shook Marjo.

"Something is in bed. What is it? It's biting me!"

"Me too," whispered her sister. "Let's call Daddy."

In a moment, barefoot Daddy was at their bedside, and in a flash he was gone again with a shout. "Hey! This place is crawling with ants!"

Hurrying back with a flashlight and his slippers, he tore open the mosquito net and yanked out the girls. Running into the other room he helped Mother brush the ants off the frightened pair. Next they rushed to put the legs of the baby's crib into cans filled with water. Then off for the insect spray.

What a battle it was! An entire band of army ants had found the house, and the girls' room, directly in their path. So they began to march right on through. Whether they actually died from the poisonous spray or drowned in it will never be known for sure. But the next morning revealed quite a sight. Dead ants were lying everywhere, and they made quite an impressive heap when they were finally swept up.

The family thanked God over and over again for his care which had helped them win the battle with the army ants.

A poisonous snake, an army of fierce ants, and now a fire!

Some things can be very frightening to children, such as being all alone, or darkness, or strange shadows. For Marjo it was fire.

She may have had reason for her fear. Another missionary family's large, grass-roofed home had recently burned to the ground. The little girl would never forget the sight of orange flames roaring through every window and door, and the heap of ashes which was all that was left when it was over.

Their own grass-roofed house was on a high hill, offering a lovely view of the countryside for miles around. Each night the darkness was polka-dotted with dozens of orange bush fires, lit by Nigerian farmers to clear their land. Some were a mile or two away, most much farther.

It became a nightly ritual, as Marjo lay in bed, for her to look anxiously through the screened windows, which were barred to keep out thieves, and to call, "Daddy, please come here."

Patiently Daddy would come into the room, knowing full well what the next question would be.

"Daddy, is that fire going to come here?"

"No, it is too far away. Now, go to sleep. Do not worry about that little fire."

But worry she did. And one day, her fears became a reality. Daddy was gone for the day, leaving Mother and the children alone. About midday they smelled smoke and noticed that a large bush fire had been started at the bottom of the hill. In no time at all the fire was raging out of control, angrily consuming the dry grass and brush in its path. Suddenly the entire hill was surrounded by fire. Mother alerted the Nigerian workers to prepare buckets of water and be ready to beat out any flames daring to come near the grass roof of their home. The grass had been kept cut very short for quite a distance around the house, to discourage both snakes and fire. Mother knew things were quite well under control, but Marjo did not.

In terror and panic she raced from one window to another. Wherever she looked there was fire! Oh, if only her father was here. She would feel so much safer. What if their roof started on fire? What if their house burned like the other family's? What if . . .? What if . . .?

Running to Mother, she threw herself into the safety of her arms. "Do not be afraid, Honey," said Mother gently. "God is taking care of us. Shall we tell him about it?"

Together they bowed their heads and asked God to keep them all safe and help the men put out the fire.

Sometime later the fire stopped as suddenly as it had begun, probably halted by the short grass and the back-fires made by the firefighters.

You can be sure that when Daddy came home that evening, he had a hard time understanding as everybody talked at once telling him about the fire. Looking at Marjo, who was snuggled safely under his arm, he asked, "And how about you?"

"Mom and I prayed," she answered, "and God put out the fire!"

12

Maijaki and the Fulanis

"The Fulanis are near Mkar again!" The word spread rapidly through the village of Mkar and through the mission boarding school there. Missionary Dik heard the news at the school and he began to think. Somehow, he must bring the good news of Jesus to the Fulanis.

The Fulani people were cattle herders. They wandered about the country in search of grazing land for their long-horned, hump-backed cows. For shelter they built simple grass huts that could easily be left when it was time to move on.

The Fulanis did not know about Jesus. Instead, they accepted Muhammad as the true prophet of God. They also lived in great fear of evil spirits. They had many rituals and charms to keep the evil spirits from harming them.

Missionaries had not visited the Fulanis, because the tribe moved from place to place so often. Also, the missionaries didn't know the Fulani language, so they couldn't talk directly to those people.

"But most of the Fulanis also understand the Hausa language," Missionary Dik thought. "Students at the mission school speak Hausa. We can use them."

The boys at the boarding school had just finished their Sunday dinner of pounded yams when Missionary Dik appeared in the doorway. "I need two of you who can speak Hausa to go with me," he said. "I would like to visit the Fulani people today."

Immediately two boys responded, "We will go with you."

So Mr. Dik and the boys began the long walk in the hot sun to the Fulani camp. With them they carried a battery-run record player and a few gospel records in the Hausa language.

At the camp, the Fulani chief greeted his visitors warmly, *"Sannun Ku! Lafia!"* Then he offered them a drink of milk. Fulani milk, the visitors knew, was always warm and tasted sour; the Fulanis had no refrigerators. And flies that followed the cows were everywhere, sometimes even floating in the milk! But it would have been impolite for visitors to refuse the offer, even if they did have a hard time drinking that milk. For the sake of Jesus, even sour milk can be downed. So the visitors drank politely.

The Fulani people were very pleased when they noticed that visitors had come. Soon a crowd gathered, eager to see the visitors and hear what they had to say.

Maijaki Usman was one of that crowd. Maijaki was a very bright fourteen-year-old Fulani boy. Once, he had gone to school for a few months and then taught himself to read the Hausa language. He had also learned a little English somewhere in his wanderings with the tribe. Now, with other members of his tribe, Maijaki came to see the visitors and hear what they had to say.

Mr. Dik did not know Maijaki and so did not single him out for special attention. He played the Hausa gos-

pel records, and the boys helped him speak in Hausa to
the crowd. To him, Maijaki was one of the crowd.

But God knew Maijaki, and God singled him out for
special attention.

Maijaki listened intently. He learned that Jesus is the
only way to God, not Muhammad as he had always
heard. Maijaki's heart was touched. Later that week he
sat down and painstakingly wrote a letter to Mr. Dik:

> To prophet or Christian man.
>
> Mr. Man, i want to write this letter to you But i don't
> know your name. i am very Happy to saw you last sun-
> day. Please sir we must try Preaching to our family Fu-
> lani because i know the places where they live. After
> that i know to preaching the gospel in our language. But
> one thing gave me trouble. becuase you are not know
> hausa language or our language Fulani. i am not know
> english well. i stop here. i'm maijaki one of the fulani
> tribe at Mkar.

So Maijaki and Mr. Dik became good friends. They
went to other Fulani camps together. Sometimes Maijaki served as translator for Mr. Dik and sometimes he
preached about Jesus Christ himself.

Since Fulanis moved often, the time Maijaki and Mr.
Dik spent together was limited. But every time the Fulanis came to the Mkar area, Maijaki came to visit and
to accompany Mr. Dik to the Fulani camps.

Several years passed. Maijaki did not lose his interest
in the gospel. He continued helping Mr. Dik teach the
Fulanis about Jesus.

But the time came for the Dik family to return to
America. Mr. Dik worried about what would happen to

Maijaki and the Fulanis when he left. How would they continue to learn about God? Mr. Dik could think of only one way. Before he left, he gave Maijaki a Bible.

Seven more years passed.

"The Fulanis are near Mkar again!" Once more the word spread rapidly through the area. Once more a missionary decided to visit them. Once more, Maijaki was in the crowd that gathered.

But this was a different crowd. The people were still Fulanis, and they were the same people that Mr. Dik had visited. But now, some of the Fulanis were Christians!

How did that happen? God had used the message Mr. Dik brought and the Bible he had given to Maijaki when he left.

Over the years, Maijaki treasured that Bible and read it often. Other Fulanis in his camp looked up to him because he was the only Fulani they knew who could read. They also wanted to learn to read. Maijaki taught them by using the Bible. And as they learned to read, many of them believed what they read. They began to realize that Jesus Christ died on the cross for the Fulanis also, and that Jesus was their savior.

Many years after Mr. Dik left, Maijaki wrote him another letter. In it he said:

> After greetings, I would like to inform you that what you planted has grown. We find that believers are increasing. The Lord Jesus is working. Our people the Fulani are always hearing the word of God. . . .

Mr. Dik used his opportunity to plant tiny seeds for Jesus. People can also plant the seeds of kindness, patience, love, or sharing in the life of someone who does not know about God's love. God can make great things happen from just a small beginning. That certainly proved true with Maijaki and the Fulanis!

13

The "Raggedy Man"

"**K**ombor! Kombor!"

Paul and Stan, aged four and six, raced across the grass, joyously shouting the name of the tall man who came down the path toward their round, mud-brick home. Kombor showed his white teeth in a big smile and spread his arms wide to catch them. They all hugged each other, laughing and wriggling until they rolled in a heap onto the ground.

Kombor was a "raggedy man." He loved children and they loved him. The boys were happy to see him whenever he came. And he came often because he was the handyman of the little mission at Sevav. When he was there, the boys loved to follow him and watch him work. There was plenty of work for him to do.

Sometimes the mud-brick walls of the missionary's house needed patching. Or the walls inside needed whitewashing. Or the well became muddy and had to be cleaned. Or the furniture had to be repaired.

Kombor had learned how to trim the orange trees and mango trees in the orchard behind the house. Often he picked the ripe fruit, put it in a basket on the missionary's bike, and pedaled down to the river and sold it.

75

Of course, Kombor was paid for his work. But the orchard belonged to the mission, so the money he got for the fruit belonged to the mission. It was never very much, but it helped pay mission expenses.

One day, Kombor began to wish that he had fruit of his own to sell so that he could keep the money. He didn't have an orchard, but there was plenty of fruit in the mission orchard. Why not take a little of that for himself, he thought, and sell it? He knew that would be stealing, but he did it anyway. And then he did it again, and again, and again.

Soon someone came to the missionary and said, "Kombor is taking fruit from the orchard and selling it. He's keeping the money."

"Oh, no," the missionary answered. "Kombor is a Christian. He wouldn't steal."

But after a while, others told the missionary the same thing. When he had watched Kombor carefully, the missionary knew it was true. Kombor was stealing! So he called Kombor into his office and asked him about it.

"No," Kombor answered. "I did not steal any fruit. I would never do that." Kombor would not admit his sin.

But the missionary was sure. He said to Kombor, "I am sorry, but we cannot have someone who steals and lies working for us. We will have to get another man in your place."

Kombor hung his head sadly and walked away. He was sorry to lose his job. The missionary was sad, too. He was sad to lose his good helper, and sad because of the sin. But Paul and Stan were the saddest of all. They loved Kombor. They were sad because Kombor had done bad things and because they would not have their "raggedy man" playmate anymore.

Yet Kombor did come to see the missionary once in

a while. He hoped the missionary would ask him to work again. But the missionary could not do that as long as Kombor did not confess his sin.

Whenever Kombor came, Paul and Stan would run to meet him just as they always had. They would all hug each other and laugh and roll in a heap on the ground, even though they were rather sad.

One time when Kombor came, he went straight to the missionary's office. The missionary saw at once that Kombor had something special on his mind. So he waited quietly until Kombor spoke.

"I did steal fruit and sell it," he confessed. "I did keep the money." He went on to tell of other bad things he had done.

"I'm sorry for my sin," Kombor finished. "But the Lord loves me! I know he loves me!"

The missionary's eyes filled with happy tears when he heard that, he was so glad Kombor confessed his sin and had found the love of Jesus again. They prayed together, praising and thanking him for turning Kombor back from sin.

Then Kombor said, "Do you know how I came to be so sure that God loves me?"

The missionary shook his head.

"It was your children," Kombor said. "They knew I had done bad things, but they were still glad to see me when I came. They always ran to meet me and shouted, 'Kombor! Kombor!' They loved me. And that's how I know that God loves me, too."

The missionary's heart was full of joy as they walked together to the house to tell the good news there. It was wonderful to know that God had used his two little boys to bring Kombor back to himself. Together, they all thanked God for his gift of love.

Through those boys God showed Kombor the most wonderful truth in all the world, that God loves sinners! "While we were yet sinners Christ died for us."

The Lost Doll

Toys are very special to missionary children. They often live in countries where there are no shopping malls and no toy stores. They can't go to a store whenever they need to buy a gift for a friend or wish to spend their allowances on something nice for themselves. These children must take special care of the toys they have. They make sure they are not left outside in the rain, or in a place where somebody could take them. The boys and girls of Nigeria, where this story takes place, do not have any toys from stores. They have only what they make themselves from old tin cans, nails, and bits of wood or grass. The toys of missionary children are unbelievably wonderful in the eyes of the Nigerian children.

And that's how Betsy was. She was just an ordinary little rubber doll with curly brown hair. But the little black boys and girls would gently touch her in wonder and then giggle in amusement and disbelief.

How Marjo loved her doll Betsy! She and her little sister spent hours playing house with their dolls in the shade of their veranda.

One afternoon Mother called the girls in from their play. "Dinnertime! Come in and wash your hands."

Running quickly to obey, Marjo left Betsy lying on the veranda. When she ran back to get her a few minutes later, Betsy was nowhere to be seen. "Mother! Where is Betsy? Did you take her inside?"

"No, I didn't. Maybe Marilee did."

With growing fear Marjo asked her sister, "Marilee, do you have Betsy?"

"No. You left her on the veranda. Isn't she there?"

Frantically Marjo and her whole family looked everywhere; there was no sign of Betsy. She had simply vanished.

Marjo was heartbroken. It was quite obvious to her that someone had been waiting for just the right opportunity to take the little doll. Betsy could be miles away in no time.

"I am going to ask Jesus to send Betsy back," said Marjo tearfully. And she did. Not once or twice, but day after day. It would have touched your heart to see her pleading with Jesus for her precious doll. When nearly two weeks had passed, both Mother and Dad tried to explain to Marjo that Jesus does not always answer our prayers with a yes. Sometimes he answers with a no. Probably that was how Jesus was going to answer her prayer this time.

And then a very strange thing happened. One day, a wrinkled old Nigerian man who worked in the yard came to the house holding something in his hand.

"Small girl," he said to Marjo in broken English, flashing her a toothless grin. "I find dis ting for tall grass. It be from you? Somebody hide it well-well."

It was Betsy!

This happened many years ago. Marjo is grown up

now and has four little girls of her own. And she still
has Betsy. The little doll is safely tucked away as a re-
minder that God really does hear and answer the prayers
of his children.

15

Nomso

The news spread rapidly from one hut to the next. All the people soon knew that Odo's second wife had borne him a baby boy. Just what he wanted! The women clapped their hands for joy and hurried to Odo's hut to see the baby. The men laughed and shouted for joy.

But Nyiwan, Odo's second wife, was very ill. Soon she died, and the sad news spread through the village. All the laughing and clapping turned to sadness, weeping and wailing.

Odo sat quietly amid the commotion. How could he take care of such a tiny baby? His first wife was too old and feeble. Besides, she had never had children of her own. The other village women felt sorry for him, but not one offered to take the baby. Each one had enough children of her own.

Odo was not a Christian, but he had heard of the clinic for mothers and babies at Lupwe. He had heard that the missionaries there were very kind and good. He loved his baby and wanted him to have good care. So he wrapped the tiny baby in brightly colored cloth and boarded a lorry (truck) to Lupwe.

Lupwe was thirty miles away. The truck, jam-packed

with people, a few goats, several chickens with their feet tied together with grass rope, and bags and boxes of all sizes, took him twenty-six dusty, bumpy miles. He had to walk the last four—carrying a very hungry little baby. He was glad when he arrived and Nurse Anita took the baby lovingly in her arms.

After exchanging greetings, Odo told Nurse Anita the whole sad story.

"*Wan ngu iti shinti* (Does your baby have a name)?" she asked in his own Tiv language.

"No," Odo answered. In his village parents did not name a baby until they were sure that the baby would live.

So the nurses named the baby Nomso. That means "man child" in the Tiv language. Odo returned to his village, content. He knew that his baby boy would have good care at Lupwe.

The nurses did take good care of Nomso. They loved him, for he was such a good baby. And once a week, Odo came to see Nomso and hold him for a little while. He was pleased with the care Nomso was receiving and he saw that his baby was growing.

Although the baby was growing, something was wrong. When Nomso was about three months old, the nurses began to worry. They could see that his head was too big and he did not watch moving things as babies usually do. Nurse Anita dangled a bright shiny toy in front of his big brown eyes, hoping he would watch it move. He didn't. "He's blind!" she whispered. "And the big head means he has water on his brain. He will never develop as other babies do."

She was sad, and so were the other missionaries. Nothing could be done for Nomso. There was no way Nomso could receive the special care he needed at the small mission station. How Nurse Anita wished there was a special hospital nearby where she could take Nomso, but there was none.

The next time Odo came to see his son, Nurse Anita told him what she was thinking. But Odo would not believe that his son was blind. He laughed about the big head and said, "My head is big too! He is like me!"

But as the weeks passed Nomso did not develop as a baby should. He did not sit up alone, or try to creep or walk. His arms and legs twisted and jerked, and he could not hold a toy. And he could not see.

One day Odo came for his usual visit. As he stood looking at his son all his love seemed to dry up. He shook his head and said, "This child means nothing to me." He left, sad and bitter. That was his last visit. He could not love his son who would not develop normally.

But Nurse Anita still loved the little boy. Although she was very busy, she took care of him. She took him to her home to be her own son. She did all she could to make him happy.

Nomso loved Nurse Anita. Although he could not see her, he could hear her when she came to his bed. When she talked to him, he answered with a crooked smile. When she tucked him in for the night, she would sing to him:

> Jesus loves Nomsie-boy, I know,
> For the Bible tells me so.
> Little ones to him belong,
> They are weak but he is strong.

Then he would smile and gurgle, as if he were trying to sing along with her.

Yes, Nomso did belong to Jesus. And when he was

eleven years old, Jesus took him home to be with him in heaven. Nurse Anita wept. She would miss him so! But she smiled through her tears, because Nomso's troubles were over at last. And she knew she would see him again!

What happened to Odo, Nomso's father? He had heard about Jesus and the salvation story many times. But, as far as we know, he never gave his heart to the Lord. And he never saw his son again.

Nurse Anita knew that Christian love is special, just as children who can't see or hear or walk are special. She knew that it was very important to show the Nigerian people that God loves all children, even handicapped ones. And so she loved little Nomso, as she knew Jesus loved him, with all her heart. Odo never knew that, although he had forsaken his son, Nomso had a Father in heaven who did love him—a Father who makes all children and loves them exactly the way they are.

16

The Treasure Chest

Mother's big brown cedar chest was full of treasures. Sara and Beth loved to look at all the pretty things Mother had neatly folded and tucked safely inside the chest. There was a beautiful hand-knit blanket, for example, which a dear friend had made for Mother as a wedding gift, and a pretty little silk baby dress all pink and white and ruffly. The two sisters loved to feel its silky softness and imagine having a baby sister to wear it. There were other things too: warm, winter sweaters and hats, new dresses to grow into, and most fun of all to see, Sara's braids! Mother had cut Sara's long blond hair several months before; but instead of throwing it all away, she had first carefully braided it. Then, tying each braid at top and bottom, she had cut them off, wrapped them up and tucked them safely into her cedar chest. Yes, mother's chest was a treasure chest indeed!

Why did Mother not store these pretty things in the closet? Sara and Beth's parents were missionaries in the faraway land of Nigeria. In that country there are lots of moths and other insects that can spoil clothes, especially warm clothes that are not worn very much. And because it is always hot in Nigeria, nobody needs warm clothes. So the safest place to keep them until they are needed for travel in colder countries is in a closed bag or a box like Mother's chest.

One day the family prepared to leave for a much-needed vacation. Dad slammed down the hood of their old Chevy. He had just finished checking the oil, gas, and tires to make sure that everything was all right. "Everybody ready? Let's go!"

"I just have to fill our canteens with drinking water," Mother answered through the screened window. "As soon as the girls finish their packing, we can go. Girls, are you about ready?"

Sara and Beth looked at their already-bulging suitcase. "I hope we haven't forgotten anything," said Beth.

"Well, let's check," replied Sara. "A game for in the car, a book for each of us, our dolls, clothes, sandals, our swimsuits . . . yup! It's all here. We're ready, Mom!"

Soon the car was loaded. Dad locked the house door securely and slid in behind the wheel. They were off at last!

A few days later their vacation came to an unexpected end. Friends arrived with bad news. "Thieves broke into your house last night. You should return home and see how much is missing."

With heavy hearts Sara and Beth helped repack the car for the return trip. Once they were on the way, they began talking about what they might find upon reaching home. Asokon, the old man who guarded the compound and their house, must have fallen asleep or he would have caught the thieves for sure. Because stealing was always a problem, all the windows had heavy bars on them for safety. Still, the bars did not always keep out unwanted intruders.

The house was a mess when they walked in. Things

were scattered here and there, drawers stood open, and dirt and glass littered the floor where the thieves had managed to break through a window. And then they realized the truth: Mother's chest was gone! It had disappeared! And with it, all the pretty things inside. Sara and Beth burst into tears.

Just then Akase, one of their Nigerian friends, knocked on the screen door. "Please, Ortese," he said to Dad, shuffling his bare feet nervously on the smooth, cement floor. "Come. See what I find."

He led the way to a spot at the bottom of the hill near their home. There, lying in the tall grass with its cover broken open, was Mother's chest! Of course there was not much left inside. The pretty blanket was gone, the soft silky dress was gone, the warm sweaters were gone. Why, even one of Sara's braids had disappeared! Akase found the other one stuck on a little bush where it must have been dropped.

"Bad man think box have money, plenty money inside," explained Akase. "He take. No find money. Throw box in *toho* (grass). Take things inside to house. *M'sugh,* I plenty sorry."

Later that evening, as Sara and Beth helped Dad light the kerosene lamps and hang them around the house for light, they thought again about the pretty things they would never see again. "Why did those thieves have to come?" Beth asked Dad with tears in her eyes.

"I think that God allowed this to happen because he wants to teach us something," replied Dad. "In fact, it reminds me of a special verse about this very thing. Here, I'll read it to you."

Taking Sara and Beth onto his lap, he opened his worn Bible to Matthew 6:19 and began to read: "Do not store up for yourselves treasures on earth, where moth and rust destroy, and where thieves break in and steal. But store up for yourselves treasures in heaven, where moth and rust do not destroy, and where thieves do not break in and steal. For where your treasure is, there your heart will be also."

"We must never love the things we have so much that they become more important to us than loving God," explained Dad. "We can store treasures in heaven by showing love to the people around us and by sharing what we have with them."

"Even if they take things without asking?" said Sara softly.

"That's right," answered Dad. "Don't let this disappointment put hatred and mean thoughts in your heart. We are here to show people who do not know about Jesus what his love is really like.

"And there is something else," continued Dad with a twinkle in his eye. "God never takes something away without giving something else in its place."

"Do you mean he will give us the same things back?" Both girls knew they could not buy any more of those pretty things in Nigeria.

"No, not necessarily," replied Dad. "But God does have a surprise for us. Look what came in the mail while we were away."

"A package! A package from America!" Now *that* was a special, rare treat. And it wasn't even Christmas!

Eagerly Sara and Beth cut the string and tore open the large cardboard box. Inside were all sorts of special treats from Aunt Gerie in far-off America: boxes of Jello, M&Ms, packets of soup, spaghetti mixes, used clothes from their cousins, coloring books, stickers, and most wonderful of all, two brand new dresses—a red one for

Sara and a blue one for Beth. And what was this? Matching doll dresses! Oh, happy day!

That package, by the way, had been on its way for several months. Wasn't it comforting that it should arrive exactly in time to remind two little girls that their father in heaven did love them very much indeed, and that his love was much more lasting than any treasure in Mother's cedar chest?

17

The Best Kind of Help

As soon as they opened their eyes that morning, Alice and Susan knew that something was wrong. Very carefully they untucked their mosquito net and slipped out of bed. They nearly bumped into Mother as she hurried past with a suitcase in one hand and a pile of clothes over her other arm.

"Oh, girls," she said as she put down her load on the kitchen table. "Bobby is very sick. Daddy and I were up most of the night with him." Bobby! Their precious baby brother! Their hearts pounded with fear.

Then they noticed Daddy kneeling by a small tub. He was holding little Bobby and pouring cool water over his feverish body. They knew that Bobby must have malaria.

Malaria is a fever carried by certain kinds of mosquitoes. Those mosquitoes are common in tropical countries like Nigeria, where this missionary family lived. They knew that any one of them might become ill with malaria; that was a risk they took living in Nigeria. But Bobby was so young and so little it especially hurt to see him suffer.

"What are you going to do?" asked Alice fearfully.

"We must get Bobby to a doctor," answered Daddy

without looking up. "Mother and I will take him to Mkar as soon as we can get ready."

Mkar, the town with the nearest mission hospital, was forty miles away. It would take at least an hour of driving on rough dirt roads to get there.

"What can we do?" Alice asked.

"You'll stay here with our friend Betty," Mother answered. "She'll look after you until Daddy returns. I'll probably stay with Bobby, but Daddy should be home by nightfall."

Without a word the sisters walked into the living room and looked at each other in despair.

"What can we do?" Alice repeated. "I want to help."

"I do, too," Susan answered. "I want to do more than just stay home. What can we do to help them?"

"I know!" Alice brightened at her idea. "We can pray!"

And so they did. Right there on the cement floor, by the old green couch, they knelt down and poured out their hearts to Jesus.

"Dear Lord, please be with Mother and Daddy as they take Bobby to Mkar. We love Bobby so much. Please be with him and make him better. Amen."

Soon Daddy and Mother were ready to go. Hand-in-hand the girls watched and waved as the car with their precious little brother drove out of sight. That evening Daddy returned alone.

The days that followed were empty without Bobby around to play with and fuss over. Time seemed to drag endlessly, time they used to fill playing with Bobby. Now they had time to spare, empty time. Oh, they would play with each other, but their games seemed not quite real. They felt hollow. Something was missing. Bobby was missing.

"What can we do?" one sister would ask.

"We can pray," the other would answer. And again they would pray together, "Dear Lord, please bring Bobby home soon. We miss him so much. Amen."

Since there was no telephone, Daddy kept in touch with Mother through the mission shortwave radio early each morning. The first thing the girls asked when they got up was, "How's Bobby?" And Daddy would answer, "Mother says he's a little better each day." They all had many questions to ask Mother. Wouldn't a telephone have been wonderful?

"What can we do?" the girls would ask Daddy every morning.

He would take them on his lap and give them each a big hug. "You are already helping by being good and by playing nicely together," he would say. "Mother will be proud of you."

"But, Daddy, what can we do to *really* help?" Alice would always ask.

And Daddy would answer, "You can pray for Bobby."

Ever so faithfully they did just that. "Dear Jesus, please be with Bobby. Please make him better. Amen."

One morning, Daddy awakened the girls with exciting news. "Guess what! Bobby is better! We can pick up him and Mother in Mkar today."

The girls were so excited they could hardly eat their breakfast. The trip to Mkar seemed to take forever, they were so anxious to get there. They kept asking, "How much longer? Are we almost there?"

At last they arrived. And soon they were taking turns holding and kissing their thinner but healthy, wiggly little brother. Jesus *had* heard their prayers.

They had wanted to help and they had done the only thing they could think of doing. They had prayed. And that was the wisest and best, the most helpful thing they could have done.

God's Gifts at Work

The night was dark, and Magani scuffled slightly as he walked. He had to feel his way along the brush-lined path to his village, Baissa. The noise he made attracted an African hunter a short way off the path. The hunter called softly, but Magani didn't hear as he scuffled. Suddenly a shot rang out, and Magani was thrown to the ground. A bullet had almost torn off his leg below his knee. Red hot pain gripped him as he lay terror-stricken and in agony.

"Miss Kooiman, Miss Kooiman! Someone has been shot!"

Margaret Kooiman, a missionary nurse in Baissa, picked up her flashlight, quickly unlocked her door and stepped out into the darkness. Outside, three people stood holding a young man whose leg dangled from his knee.

"Take him to the clinic at once," she ordered. "I'll see what I can do."

In the clinic she examined Magani's shattered leg and tried to stop the blood pouring from it. She knew immediately what she should do.

"I must cut off the bottom part of his leg," she told

the anxious Nigerians gathered around her. "That's the only way to close the wound properly and stop the blood from flowing." Then she added a prayer: "Dear Lord, please help me save this young man. Guide my hands. My work and his life are in your hands."

Nurse Kooiman worked through the rest of the still, hot night. Beads of sweat dripped down her face as she worked. By the flickering light of the kerosene lamp she could see anxious faces surrounding her, but no one spoke. She heard only Magani's gasping breaths. And with every breath she worked faster, trying to save the life in her hands.

As dawn crept into the clinic, she bandaged what remained of the leg. Then she looked up at the people who had been watching. "He is still alive," she reported, "but he's very weak. He needs more surgery and more medical help than I can give him at this clinic. He must be moved to the mission hospital at Takum."

How could she contact the hospital for help? The clinic had no phone, and the radio transmitter they usually used was out for repairs. And how could they move Magani? Certainly he would not survive the long bumpy trip to Takum in a car or lorry. Nurse Kooiman had an idea.

"The mission plane is supposed to return our radio transmitter this morning," she said. "We can use the plane to take Magani to the hospital. And we can use the radio transmitter to call ahead and tell them."

The plane arrived midmorning, and Nurse Kooiman ran out to meet it. Quickly she told the pilot about the accident and explained what they needed.

"Bring out the patient," said Mr. Browneye, the missionary pilot. "I'll take him to Takum right away." So they gently placed Magani, limp and half-conscious, in the plane. Before they took off, the missionaries prayed, as they always did, for a good flight. And they asked God to spare Magani's life.

As soon as they were in the air, Mr. Browneye contacted his wife on the airplane's radio. He knew she would be waiting at the radio in Takum to hear when the plane was returning.

"Aen to Takum. Do you read me?" he called, using the name of the plane.

"Roger. Go ahead, Aen."

Mr. Browneye was thankful to hear his wife's voice. "We have a medical emergency," he said. "Please contact the hospital and have someone meet the plane. The patient must be taken to the hospital immediately."

The air was rough that morning, and Magani groaned as the plane bumped up and down. He tried to sit up in his seat; he lifted his head and strained to look around him. But he soon sank back, closed his eyes and lay without moving.

Mr. Browneye glanced at him. It was obvious that Magani had already lost a lot of blood and now was bleeding again. "Just lie still. We'll have you at a hospital soon," Mr. Browneye tried to reassure him.

Fifteen minutes later the plane rolled to a stop at the Takum airstrip. A waiting car quickly drove up to the plane, and Mrs. Browneye jumped out of the car to help. A Nigerian helper and the Browneyes gently removed Magani from the plane and laid him on the back seat of the car. Immediately the car sped off to the hospital.

"We need blood! They're bringing in a young man with a gunshot wound, and he's losing a lot of blood. We need blood!" The word had spread through the mission hospital before Magani arrived. Several Nigerian workers had donated some of their own blood to help the man.

As soon as the car arrived at the hospital, nurses ran out to carry Magani inside. Minutes later he received the blood he needed so desperately.

Soon after that, Magani began to regain strength. The doctors operated on his leg once more, and what was left slowly began to heal. Finally the doctors could say, "Magani will get better and will leave the hospital. Magani will live!"

Magani's parents were pagans. From them he had learned to worship spirits and make animal sacrifices. But at Takum hospital he heard something different, day after day. He heard about Jesus' love. He saw it in the loving care of the doctors and nurses. God had been good to Magani through the missionaries. Before he left the hospital, Magani said to the Nigerian chaplain, "When I go home I will go to a Christian church." Magani, whose name meant "medicine," had discovered that the only medicine for the sickness of sin was the Jesus he had learned about at the mission hospital.

It all began with a dark night and a gunshot wound. Magani would have died not knowing about Jesus. But God used a missionary nurse, a tiny mission clinic, a missionary pilot, a small airplane, a hospital, Nigerian Christian workers, and many Christians in other countries faithfully praying for these missionaries and supporting them. All these people worked together. They used the gifts God had given them to help save a young man's life and to show him the way to have life forever with Jesus.

God has given each one of his children certain talents and gifts. He made everyone for the special purpose of showing others he loves them just as he loved Magani.

The Hands that Helped

1

Gerard Terpstra originally told the story of "Kpa se-nongo" in *The Banner* of October 25, 1974. The story was rewritten slightly and its title changed for publication here.

Gerard Terpstra was a teacher, pastor, and writer in Nigeria from 1954 to 1969. He worked for the NKST (Church of Christ in the Sudan among the Tiv). He now lives in Grand Rapids, Michigan.

2

Neal Eldrenkamp contributed "Two Old Women and Two Small Yams." Neal's story did not include the young boy David. Neal had gone with Dr. Kremer and had received the yams. Marjo Rouw added David and the details of his life from her own experience.

Neal Eldrenkamp lived in Jos, Nigeria, from 1982 through 1984 and worked as a volunteer in media production for New Life For All. Since then he has pursued a degree in communications at Wheaton College. He now lives in Denver, Colorado, and is interested in further mission service overseas.

3

The story of Josie is told essentially as it was given us by Dianne Termorshuizen. Dianne lived in Nigeria with her family from 1972 through 1979 and from 1982 through 1986. She has always been involved in women's Bible studies and has assisted the mission in various volunteer activities while her husband served as an administrator. The Termorshuizens now live in Smithville, Ontario.

4

Marjo Rouw told the story of a friend in the kitchen from her own experience. Marjo grew up as the daughter of missionary parents in Nigeria. She attended Hillcrest School in Jos and returned to the United States for her college education. She married Otto Rouw, and they returned to Nigeria in 1974. There they served first as houseparents at Hillcrest School, and then as directors of the NKST bookshop ministry in Makurdi until 1986. The Rouws now live with their four daughters in Mt. Vernon, Washington.

5

Betty Vanden Berg sent us the facts of "A New Suit for Alu." Betty taught at the Sevav Girls School in Zaki Biam, Nigeria, from 1946 through 1954. Then she studied nursing in the United States, received her degree, and returned to Nigeria as a nurse. She has since retired and now lives in Grand Rapids, Michigan.

6

Marjo Rouw wrote "Stuck in the Stream" from her own experience.

7

Gerard Terpstra originally told the story of "The Prisoner" in *The Banner* of February 24, 1967. Although the circumstances and the main facts of the story are true, certain details have been added here to make it read smoothly.

8

"A Surprise from God" was also contributed by Gerard Terpstra and appeared in shorter form in *The Banner*, November 1, 1974. Background material for this story was furnished by Peter Bulthuis.

Peter Bulthuis taught and served as principal at Mkar Teachers' College in Mkar, Nigeria, from 1955 through 1970. While at Mkar, he also served as the general secretary for the mission in Nigeria. He now lives in Lynden, Washington.

9

Although the characters in "A Time for War" are imaginary, the circumstances and the events are real. They were furnished by Marjo Rouw, who lived through the war and whose father was the missionary at the bridge.

10

Fran Boer contributed the story of "Lydia." Fran went to Nigeria with her husband in 1966. They lived in Wukari and Baissa, where she taught Bible in national schools. While in Wukari, the Boers took Lydia into their home and raised her as a daughter along with their own three children. The Boers now live in Jos, where Fran teaches English and Hausa at Hillcrest School.

11

Marjo Rouw wrote "Snakes, Ants, and Fire" from her own experiences in Nigeria.

12

Ralph Dik contributed the facts of "Maijaki and the Fulanis." Ralph taught in Zaki Biam, Nigeria, and at the Teachers' College in Mkar from 1956 through 1965. In 1988, he retired from Grand Rapids Christian High School.

13

The story of "The Raggedy Man" was originally written by Gerard Terpstra and published under another title in *Bible Truth*. Although the facts remain true, it has been rewritten for publication here.

14

Marjo Rouw wrote "The Lost Doll" from her own experience.

15

Anita Vissia contributed the story of "Nomso." Anita worked for thirty-five years as a nurse in Nigeria, where she took a special interest in leprosy patients. She lived in Baissa for many years, and later moved to Takum. She is now retired and lives in Grand Rapids, Michigan.

16 & 17

Both "The Treasure Chest" and "The Best Kind of Help" were written by Marjo Rouw from her own experiences.

18

Ray Browneye contributed "God's Gifts at Work." Ray served in Nigeria for twenty-three years as a builder, pilot, and administrator. He lived with his family at Lupwe, Nigeria. Now he lives in Grand Rapids, Michigan, and pilots a plane for a denominational air service.

All of the stories you have read here are true. Some details have been added to make the mission field come alive for you, but the truth of each story remains unchanged: God holds his children in his hands and directs their ways.

All of the people listed here, along with the people mentioned in the stories, have felt God's hand in very special ways. They have passed these stories on for you to realize what they have felt: you can go anywhere and do anything for God, if you keep your hand in his.